Christmas 1983

Dear Denise,

This is a spiritual book that is
to be read a "little at a time,"
meditated on, and put into practice
in your own life. Remember the
Bible is <u>the</u> spiritual book. Read
it often.

We must feed our souls with good
thoughts. It is just as important
as feeding our bodies with the
right kind of food. A well-feed
soul and body work best together
as we travel life's journey to
eternity.

Your loving Grandmother,

S. M. C.

D1570650

FRIENDS AREN'T
KEPT WAITING

More from "My Changeless Friend"

by **FRANCIS P. LE BUFFE, S.J.**
Adapted by Catharine Hughes

ARENA LETTRES • NEW YORK

Original edition published in 1949 by the Apostleship of
Prayer

Imprimi potest: John J. McMahon, S.J.

Nihil obstat: John M. A. Fearns, S.T.D.
            Censor Librorum

Imprimatur: ✠ Francis Cardinal Spellman, D.D.
            Archbishop of New York

Copyright © 1975 by Arena Lettres

Library of Congress Catalog Card Number: 75-21392

ISBN: 0-88479-000-2

———————

Printed in the United States of America

Contents

FRIENDS AREN'T KEPT WAITING   1

LIFT UP YOUR HEARTS!   2

RUDE TO GOD   4

GOD WANTS TO BE LOVED   6

PLEASE DON'T LEAVE ME ALONE   8

DOING THE THINGS OF GOD   11

PLAYING OUR OWN PART   13

YOU'RE HUNGRY   15

IN SPITE OF IT ALL   17

IT'S MY FAULT   19

UNPOPULAR   21

COMFORT TO FRIENDS   23

MAKING PEOPLE GRATEFUL   25

CONFIDANTS   27

THROWN RIGHT UP AGAINST GOD   29

MISPLACED CONFIDENCE   31

WITHOUT CHRIST—A FAILURE   33

LOVE TO THE END   35

RESTLESS FOR GOD   36

THE PLEASANTEST OF TASKS   38

A LOVER'S WAY   40

THE UNKNOWN GOD   42

TUCKING TROUBLES AWAY   43

BORROWING FUN   45

A FRIEND IN NEED   47

WHEN I'M THROUGH, I'M THROUGH   49

A FRIEND'S MEANNESS   51

SEEING BUT NOT ENTERING IN   53

LIFE'S UPS AND DOWNS 56

DEAD DREAMS IN THEIR EYES 58

KEEPING THE PAST IN MIND 60

GOD MADE ME PURPOSELY 62

FALL IN LOVE WITH GOD 64

AN EPIC OUT OF TWO GRUNTS 67

LIVING OUR LESSONS 69

MY FRIEND'S FRIENDS 71

SAYING THANK YOU 72

CHANGE THE SIGN 74

HE IS ALWAYS NEAR 76

HAPPY AND FORGETFUL 78

UPS AND DOWNS 80

ENCOURAGEMENT 82

RESCUED 84

IF ONLY . . . ! 87

GOD DOES NOT HOLD OUT ON US 89

A FRIEND'S WISHES 91

A FORGIVING SPIRIT 93

LOVED 95

HURT FEELINGS 97

INTERESTED IN OTHERS 99

A FRANK FRIEND 101

THE END IS LONG IN COMING 103

A CONSTANT VISITOR 105

SEEKING HELP RIGHTLY 107

I HOPE I DIE BEFORE YOU 109

GOD'S 111

SADNESS NOT FOR MAN 113

INDISPENSABILITY 115

THANK GOD, I KNEW HIM 117

FRIENDS AREN'T
KEPT WAITING

Look, I am standing at the door, knocking.
REVELATION 3:20

It is impolite to keep anyone waiting, above all a friend. Custom, sanctioned by the best instincts of man, teaches that, and when it is one we love and who reciprocates our love, then there must be no delay in attending to his wish. Once his voice is heard, once the sound of his feet is near, we hurry to lessen the distance that separates us.

Christ also stands at our door and knocks, not at the door of our earthly home, for that pleasure is denied us, but at our hearts. Jesus, our God, our friend from a time long before we had an earthly friend, asks us to let Him come and rest within. He comes not once or twice but daily and hourly. He asks the deepest love we have, asks it as though he could not claim the right to it. He pleads for it as a lover pleads for another's love, Yet, we keep Him knocking at our hearts. He may already be there with His sanctifying grace, but there is an inner gateway to which He would gain entrance. He has a share of our love, but has He all? Is there not a corner, perhaps a large corner, of our hearts that we are reluctant to yield to Him? Does he not often find reluctance in our giving? Hesitancy. He may ask that we sacrifice a friend who, though not actually bad, is leading us apart from our truest Friend. Here and in lesser ways, a bit of selfishness has laid a

1

claim to our hearts, a quest for ease has won an unholy conquest, a too close regard for what is temporal has kept our Lord from His full possession. They may be trifles, but they are not trifles if they make us impolite to God!

ও

Jesus, most relentless lover our human hearts have ever known, I must not, will not, withhold from You the love You crave so deeply. My heart is Yours from this hour on, Yours whole and undivided. Yet, dearest Lord, because I know my truant self, I beg Your grace so that, when You ask the sacrifices that must always be, You will not ever find me wanting.

LIFT UP
YOUR HEARTS!

Lift up your hearts! We have lifted them up to the Lord.
PREFACE OF THE MASS

Each morning, as he stands on the inner threshold of the great Sacrifice, the priest, with arms upraised, cries out: "Lift up your hearts!" There is a quick response: "We have lifted them up to the Lord." Thus it was hundreds of years ago; thus it is today; thus it will be until the end.

Yet, we must pause and ask ourselves: Can I each morning answer in the same way? Yes, we have lifted up our hearts. A new-won prize for which we had striven hard made our hearts leap when we found it within our grasp. There was a kind word from a friend, a bit of approval from another. Our hunger for sympathy was met and we were buoyed up with new courage. We found one of the little things that please—most of us have few big things—and we pressed from it an ounce of cheer. But then? Did we think of the Giver? Did our minds even once turn to the Father in Heaven from whom each good thing descends? It is so easy—yet so unmannerly—to snatch the gift and never once say "Thank you" to the Giver.

When love comes from those nearest and dearest to us, we must look beyond it to that infinite love of which it is but a spark. When comfort and encouragement come from friends who know how to feed new strength into our hearts, we must remember Him who sent the "Comforter" to give us of the seven-fold gifts and make us "strong and perfect Christians and soldiers of Jesus Christ." When another stands near us in time of trial and shores us up lest we fall, we must remember that it was our changeless Friend who bore our iniquities and died for our sins and dwells always on our altars to help us.

It will not rob us of the passing joys if we "lift our hearts up to the Lord." It will not deprive us of any of their sweetness. Instead, it will add to them. Love, sanctified by being linked to infinite love, is the truest love. Courage linked to Omnipotence will know no fear. Encouragement blessed by the Comforter will gain immeasurably.

The shadows fall too often and the clouds gather too fast at times, and they may darken our lives and make us see only gloom. But there is sunshine in back of the cloud. The shadow itself always comes because of light. And so we must learn to travel to the point where the brightness begins. That is what we do when we lift up our hearts to the Lord.

ॐ

Dear Jesus, I am so apt to catch the little joys of life and center my heart on them and to let the shadows of life cast their darkness too lingeringly. I ought to lift up my heart, but lift it also and always up to You. If I do so, it will stay lifted up for, whether joys come or go, deep in my heart will be the peace that You provide, "God of peace and all consolation."

RUDE TO GOD

Let your words be for the improvement of others, as occasion offers, and do good to your listeners, otherwise you will only be grieving the Holy Spirit of God who has marked you with his seal for you to be set free when the day comes.

EPHESIANS 4:30

The last thing a decent man or woman wants to do is to insult a guest. It is a primary dictate among all who have the least desire to be polite and who have even a minimum regard for friends. To invite a man into my house, to have him sit at my table and chat and then to do something that pains him is unthinkable.

Unthinkable at least among human friends and human acquaintances—but not when dealing with our Heavenly Guest, the Holy Ghost. By reason of sanctifying grace, we became the temple of the Holy Ghost and God resides within us in a special way. He is more truly and intimately our guest and we His host than could ever be between earthly friends. He is with us at all times whether we are at home or away, with us when we pray and when we while away the hours, with us when things are bright and when they are dark. He is with us always, a protection until the day when we are "set free," when we become His guest for all eternity.

And yet we do grieve Him when we follow lowered ideals and listen to the call of the world. And if we pamper ourselves and yield to sensuality, permitting the demands of ease and comfort to hold sway, we grieve Him then, for He is a pure Spirit and would win us to a loftier seeking. If we are unkind and hurt another, we grieve Him there, for He loves the one we hurt just as much as He loves us. If we permit our minds to wander when we pray, that impoliteness, too, is a source of grief.

With our firm faith we do not realize it. In fact, it hardly ever dawns on us that by our sins, even the slightest, we are positively rude to our Heavenly Guest.

ह॰

Dear Jesus, I am sorry that I have been so rude in the past, but I had not really thought of it all in just that light. I dislike being rude to anyone, much less being rude to God. And so I now beg pardon of You and of God the Father and of the Holy Ghost whom I have grieved, and I promise to try not to be rude again.

GOD WANTS
TO BE LOVED

The proof that you are sons is that God has sent the Spirit of his Son into our hearts: the Spirit that cries, "Abba, Father."
                                                     GALATIANS 4:6

"You know, I almost came to hate God," the young woman said. "Every time my teacher spoke of God it was: 'God will punish you if you do that.' If the priest gave a sermon, it was filled with hell and sin and God's wrath. If I asked for a prayer for some intention, I was told I might get it 'if it is God's holy will.' I was warned to expect refusal. I never once was told to pray expectant of an answer. Hearing that doesn't make you feel like working for God. There's no love in that."

"No, there isn't," said the old priest. "And it's entirely the wrong way to look at God. I couldn't serve God either if that were all I knew about Him. God is more than that."

They sat talking for a long time, until the love of God eventually warmed a heart that had almost turned against Him. And, as night fell, she went forth with a light and joy in her heart that it had never known before.

Why should we talk of God as though He were some big policeman just waiting to catch us doing something wrong? Why should all our talk be of sin and hell and God's punishments? Of course God hates sin. Of course He punishes sin. But that is not the side we ought to stress.

Life is hard enough and its burdens weigh us down sufficiently without our making it worse with a cringing fear of God. God is our *Father*. We are his *children*. Christ is our *brother*. We are not strangers, but fellow-citizens of the saints, members of the household of God. Why can't we dwell on *that*? Love drives out fear; it drives us on to the hardest things with a song on our lips. It makes all things easy.

God *is* love. He *does* love me. He loved me from the beginning and drew me out of nothing, giving me my existence. He has loved me every moment of my existence. He has so loved me that He came down from Heaven and suffered and died to save me from sin. He has so loved me that when I sinned again and again, He forgave me each time and gave me back His friendship, which I had spurned. He loves me so much that He has become my Food times without number. He dwells within me as in His tabernacle.

Love! That is what is written largest across all the dealings of God with me. Why do I not then write it boldly across all my dealings with Him? Of course we should not lose our filial fear of God any more than a loving son forgets his respectful reverence for a devoted father. But if God wished me to fear Him with a servile fear and stand in dread of Him, would He have acted as He has? If He wished me to fear Him in that way, would He have been born a babe at Bethlehem or have called to Himself all that "labor and are burdened"? If He wished me to fear Him thus, would He have told me that He was "meek and humble of heart" and that "the bruised reed He shall not break"?

It just doesn't make any sense! Yet, many do thus fear and dread God, and many talk and write and preach about Him as though He were some tyrant gloatingly waiting to cheat us of what we want, someone hungrily watching to trap us in wrongdoing. What an injustice to the God of love!

Fear cramps and numbs and repels. Love opens up the heart and unites lover with loved one. Life's road is hard enough without making it harder, harder than God ever intended it to be. Love makes it easy—or at least easier. And it is my love that God wants: "Thou shalt *love* the Lord thy God." "If you *love* Me, keep My commandments." "By this shall all men know that you are My disciples, if you have *love* one for another."

ॐ

Dear Jesus, teach me this secret of loving You. I know that You are just and that You hate sin and that You will punish it. But that is only when I force You to it. The one thing You have done is to show Your *love* for me, from the beginning down to this very moment. I wish to love You and I know that You wish to be served in a spirit of love. And that, after all, is the only decent way to serve You, isn't it?

PLEASE DON'T LEAVE ME ALONE

And know that I am with you always; yes, to the end of time.

MATTHEW 28:20

"Pray hard for me and please, please, don't leave me alone!" The words sped across the country from one who was finding the fight of life hard. Years of slight ups and hard downs had at length brought home a rightful distrust of self and, as the daily pressure and temptation closed in and he saw the same old sins so frighteningly near, he called out pleadingly. The battle must not be lost, and yet, to feel that no human help was near, help that would make the inner help of grace visible, would spell defeat, just as it had spelled it many times before. "Pray hard for me," the letter read. "Please, please, don't leave me alone."

It was a cry from one human heart, but it is also the cry that goes up constantly from anyone who has his soul's safety constantly in mind. There is an open danger here, a hidden snare there, a beguiling allurement elsewhere, and even when they are gone there are old cravings of mind and heart and body which would lead us away from God. Man's life is truly a warfare and he cannot fight alone.

And why? Simply because it is hard to push ahead when there is no one at your side. It is hard to give and take in the game of life and never have anyone to tell you: "Well done!" It is hard to wipe away the tear and wear a deceiving smile if no one has seen the tear fall and no one pierces beneath the mask. It is hard to walk through the valley of the shadow of death and know that, if in a moment of slipping we were to reach out our hand for help, it would fall back untouched to our side.

"It is not good for man to be alone" is as true today as it was when the first man walked in

Eden. Deep within us is the yearning for someone who will guide and guard us, who will lift up our drooping eyes until we can again see "the mountains whence cometh help." At times, we are joyful and unconscious of this craving, reveling in the merrymaking and the music of the moment. But let the music be hushed, let the shadows fall, and the old gnawing is there again in full consciousness. We are alone.

No, not unless we wish to have it so.

No matter where we are, no matter when this need for help is felt, there is One to whom we can turn, One whose very nearness robs the desert of its loneliness, One whose absence would make a throng of thousands an utter isolation. He is ever ready and most willing to take us by the hand and help us over the rough places and through the gathering darkness, to protect us against danger, whether it is obvious or hidden. But we must call upon Him and we must ask His help. He has willed it thus, that we ourselves should show care for our souls. We must cry out to Him: "Please, Lord, don't leave me alone!"

ᢒᜰ

Dear Lord, I need You much in this brief struggle we call life. I really want to win the fight and be a credit to the saving power of Your grace. But You know how weak I am, and I know it too. My own past makes me rightly afraid of myself—afraid, too, of "invasion and of the noon-day devil." And so I beg You now to give me much grace so that in every hour of need I may cry from my heart, "Please, please, don't leave me alone!" And, please, hearken always quickly to my cry.

DOING THE THINGS OF GOD

Why do you call me, "Lord, Lord" and not do what I say?

LUKE 6:46

The people were all gathered about our Lord on the plain in Galilee and they were being told plain truths. One charge after another was laid on them, kindly but firmly, and then, as though summing up the whole situation, our Lord said plainly: "Why do you call me, 'Lord, Lord' and not do what I say?" He knew that the poor people followed Him and that they hungered for a leader. He could not help hearing their many protestations of loyalty and devotion. Yet, He has but one straightforward answer to it all. Words are cheap; words, though well-meant, are passing things that cost little. Deeds tell, for they cost. Solid proof of loyalty lies in deeds, not in words.

Our Lord spoke those words long, long ago, but He meant them for each and every one of us. We all call Him "Lord, Lord"; but do we do the things that He says? No matter in what sphere we live, God's will is written large there. And if we neglect the known will of God or fail to search for it when we are in doubt, then all our cries of love and all our protestations of devotion are sounding brass and tinkling cymbals.

Father and mother have clear, definite duties to each other and to their children. If these are neglected—no matter how holy the pretense—all

11

the extra prayers and activities and pious associations are but cries of "Lord, Lord" with the proof of our love wanting.

Children owe much to parents and if these duties are left unfulfilled all other good works, all holy practices, are vain delusions, for the essentials of their state of life are absent.

It is the same in the business world. It is all well and good to be generous with the money we have made. But have we earned it justly? It is a vain cry of "Lord, Lord" when our money goes ostentatiously to help the starving if that same money has been made off others who starve and to whom we sell our products or employ for a meager salary.

Teachers and all those who have charge over others have much here with which to challenge themselves. Long prayers are excellent. But have class assignments been prepared well and the students' work been corrected? Spiritual work with students outside of class is good, but is the ordinary, humdrum, colorless routine work also done right? The "Lord, Lord" of these "extras" is good enough, but are we doing the routine things, the essential things that He wants, and which are demanded if good work is to be done?

ॐ

Dear Lord, I know myself and what strange notions can and do come to me. When I think of sanctity and of serving You well, my mind at once turns toward extra prayers, extra work, extra activities. I am too prone to stress the unusual and to forget that real love of You is shown first of all and principally in doing what You want me to do when You want me to do it. This is mostly so colorless and lacking in thrills that I instinctively reach out for the unusual. And yet I must learn this fundamental lesson and learn it soon. So give me grace, of course, to say "Lord, Lord," but at the same time to show You that I mean it by doing the things that You say.

PLAYING OUR OWN PART

Saul was very angry; the incident was not to his liking. "They have given David the tens of thousands," he said, "but me only the thousands."

1 SAMUEL 18:8

"The grass is always greener, you know, in the other fellow's yard," he said. It was the only answer that could be given to the petulant outpourings of jealousy that had come so spitefully from the woman's lips. "Some other part in the play should have been given to me—that's all." "Well, what if it should?" he responded. "Why let that make you botch the part you have? Why be so jealous as to make yourself behave this way? Stop stamping your feet in anger and look to your own part and do that well. The grass is always greener. . . ."

We are such fools at times! Instead of trying to manage what we have, instead of measuring up to tasks assigned or bearing the crosses that have been placed on us, we turn our envious eyes to others and keep repeating to ourselves, "Oh, if only I were like that!"

A young man and woman stand at the altar, hand in hand in marriage, pledging to share whatever the years may bring. But, as time passes and others reap more plentifully of the fruits of the world—of money, honors and pleasures—they feel a tugging at their hearts and perhaps bitterness begins to grow. They fail to count upon the favors God has bestowed upon them. They forget to total up the good things He has given them. "The grass is greener" over there and so they spoil the part God would have them play in life.

Here is a young man who had high ambitions, who wished to stand out before all men in terms of his attainments and success. Yet God, for His own reasons, may have sealed the doors fast shut and denied all entrance there. Of course it is hard to make a great detour in life and to come out far away from our self-plotted path. But if God wants it so, are we going to be forever gazing elsewhere than at the tasks assigned us here and now? Shall we childishly pout and stamp our feet because we cannot do what we want?

The tasks of life await us daily, hourly, and we would be very wise to take them as they are. They might have been otherwise, of course, and they might have been more to our liking. But what of that? A hundred years from now it will make no difference whether we have stood high or low, whether we did big things or the very small ones that are the essence of most men's lives. What will matter then is the manner of the doing. That will mean everything. Not the "what" but the "how" of our lives is what will count.

෫ক

Dear Jesus, You know what a jealous person I am. I am always wanting to be otherwise, always grieving because I am not called to play the part in life that others play. It is childish, but it is true, much as it hurts me to admit it. So please let me learn to stop this yearning to play another's part and give me the sense to attend to myself and to my own affairs, the sense to use all my energy to play my own part well.

YOU'RE HUNGRY

At that time there was a severe famine.
1 MACCABEES 9:24

The bus was moving down Broadway. In the seat behind me two women were carrying on a conversation. Above the noise, their voices carried to my ears. One of the women was very querulous and made repeated curt remarks. Finally, her companion said, kindly but firmly, "Do you know what's the matter with you? You're hungry."

"You're hungry." As I looked out on Broadway, a thought flashed across my mind: "Poor men and women! The matter with you is that you're hungry, very hungry. That's why you are restless and always on the go. That's why you draw out your revels almost till the dawn. That's why you keep feeding yourselves more and more pleasure. You're hungry, but not with a physical hunger that you can assuage with the good things of life. It is a ceaseless, gnawing hunger of the soul. And the pleasures you so constantly seek only make you hungrier. You're hungry—hungry for God!"

Long ago, Saint Augustine cried: "Our souls are made for Thee, O God, and they are restless till they rest in Thee." Not all the pleasant things of life are bad, nor are they worthless. But they simply cannot give ultimate satisfaction. A piece of candy pleases a child for a while; a toy amuses him for the moment. A dance can bring real pleasure while it lasts and a party can speed the hours away quite joyfully. But all these are passing. When they are gone our souls are hungrier than ever.

That is why from our earliest years the Church tries to tell us of God and of His love for us. That is why she points to the pleasant things of earth, too, and blesses them. Yet, even as she does so, she gives her warning that these things are good only because they are intended to lead us to something better. She blesses man and woman with marriage and hallows it, but she also lifts their eyes beyond the world of sense and focuses them on Christ. She takes young children into her classrooms and instructs them, but also tells them of God, Who is truth itself and in Whom all lesser truths find their meaning.

સ✦

Dear Jesus, my soul is often a puzzle to me. It is so restless at times. Some of the pleasures it reaches for I need, and some of them I can rightly have. But they leave me wanting something else. Sometimes, the call of sin is loud and its pleasures are blatant in their appeal. Stand by me then, dear Lord, and make me clearly see that all such earthly foods will always leave me hungry.

IN SPITE OF IT ALL

*Though your sins are like scarlet, they shall
be as white as snow; though they are red as
crimson, they shall be like wool.*

ISAIAH 1:18

"Yes, every word of it is true. He is mean;
he is selfish; he is untruthful. Gratitude has no
place in his make-up and politeness and con-
sideration are unknown to him. He has treated
me shamefully and has no use for the children.
All that and more is true—but in spite of it I love
him." Thus the frail, tired little woman spoke
from her heart.

It's wonderful, we say. Yes, it is, but there is
an even more wonderful love than that in the
world. It is the love of God for our wayward, self-
centered hearts. "Can a woman forget her in-
fant, so as not to have pity on the son of her
womb? And if she should forget, yet will not I
forget thee. Behold, I have graven thee in My
hands." That is the story of God's dealings with
mankind; that is the story of His dealings with
each soul; that is the story of His dealings with
my own soul. Despite my past with all its negli-
gence and frequently repeated sins, our Lord cries
out to me: "In spite of it all I love you."

Our past is one long record of transgressions.
Scarcely had we come to know of the gift of our
baptismal innocence than we began to use our
newly-won reason to flaunt His law. Our own will
was very sweet to us, far more enticing than the
strict way of His commandments. Childish will-

17

fulness soon grew into youthful self-seeking and a
gross disregard of much that He would want became larger in our lives. Then, when the years
had brought us to full maturity, though they
took away with them the outward manner of children, there still remained rebellion against God's
law. With regard to Him alone, childhood's un-
disciplined ways still prevailed.

Perhaps there have been few mortal sins in
our lives, but what a mess of self-seeking and petty
vanities and lack of decent respect for the reasonable wishes of others! Perhaps we did kneel each
morning and each evening in prayer, but what
little regard we had for politeness when it was
God with whom we spoke! We went to church
quite frequently, perhaps, but did we pay as much
attention as we did when we went to the movies?

It may be that we have all too frequently violated God's law in serious ways. Perhaps sin has
come into our lives in ways that we thought could
never occur. Perhaps the story of the prodigal has
been rewritten in our own behavior and we have
tried to feed our souls on the husks of swine, far
from our Father's home.

Yet, regardless of the past, as we turn to our
Lord we hear Him cry: "In spite of it all, I love
you." In spite of it all! Why? Because He made
us from utter nothingness and called us into being "in His own image and likeness"; because He
redeemed us, paying our ransom with his own
Precious Blood; because He has sanctified us time
and again, whenever we gave Him the chance to
draw us unto Him. In spite of it all! Because He
sees all the good we can do—for ourselves, for
others, for Him—and He is quite too big to be

done with us and let us have our own way in spoiling things.

~

Dear changeless Friend, how wonderfully insistent You are in Your love for me! I do not deserve it at all. I have done enough to spoil any love for me, yes, any love except Yours. My past is enough to disgust anyone with me, if it were known as You know it. But not so with You. "In spite of it all I love you." Dear Lord, too long, too very long, have You been forced to put it that way. So now I beg You, please give me much grace that soon, very soon, You may drop those words: "In spite of it all."

IT'S MY FAULT

Jerusalem, Jerusalem, you that kill the prophets and stone those who are sent to you! How often have I longed to gather your children, as a hen gathers her chicks under her wings, and you refused!
                                     MATTHEW 23:37

There was one thing that the Jews could never say with any truth and that was that Christ did not try to win their love. Time and time again He insisted that it was to them first that He must preach the Kingdom of God. It was in their towns that He had cured the sick and the lame and the blind. It was on their lake that He had stilled the

storm and swept the fishes miraculously into their
nets. To Jerusalem He had come again and again,
teaching in its streets, crying out in its Temple.
Pleading He had come, scolding He had come,
with a whip of cords He had come—but Jerusalem
would have none of it: "Jerusalem, Jerusalem . . .
how often have I longed to gather your children
. . . and you refused!"

Jerusalem could not truthfully blame our
Lord, and neither can I. If I am not holier today
than I am, the fault is all my own. His grace has
been plentiful in my life and He has never denied me any grace that I needed. Jerusalem killed
the prophets and stoned them that had been sent
by God as bearers of His message. It murdered
them despite God's plentiful graces given her children to understand and hearken to His call. I,
too, may have sinned, sinned grievously and frequently and defiantly. This I did despite the grace
He gave me at every moment of my life. It was
my own willfulness that caused my sin. The sin
was mine and I fell, rejecting the grace which
came plentifully into my soul.

And, after I had sinned, He again pleaded with
me for my love. If I did not give Him my love,
it was *I* who refused *Him*.

No, I can never blame our Lord. He has been
very, very good to me. And I? To put it on the
lowest level, I have been grossly impolite, refus-
ing to open the door of my heart when He stood
there knocking.

But that is in the past and it must not discourage me. Of course, I ought to be ashamed; I
ought to be thoroughly sorry. But discouraged, no.
For He forgives and forgets and, right now, He

is pleading for my love just as though I had never treated Him as I have.

ॐ

Dear Jesus, I am thoroughly ashamed of myself for the way I have treated You. No day has passed without Your grace coming plentifully. Yet, I have steadily refused to give You my love and when I did give it, I gave it quite grudgingly. It is so mean and ungrateful of me that it would discourage me if I did not know that You love me despite it all. I am sorry, but not discouraged. With Your grace, I will do better in the future.

UNPOPULAR

I stay awake, lamenting like a lone bird on the roof.

PSALMS 101:7

"The only unpopular person at that place was Jesus Christ," was the short and biting description given of a certain summer resort. Every other home was visited again and again, but few feet strayed across the threshold of Christ's door. In every other house there was the sound of music and of laughter far into the night, but where the Friend of mankind dwelt, there, and there alone, did night hold her silence. In all that restless town there were no lonely ones thinking away the twilight hours, save One who long years back had trod the wine-press of Olivet alone and even yet must watch out many a day and night com-

panionless. Often indeed might our Lord have repeated to Himself:

> Face on face in the city, and when will
> the faces end,
> Face on face in the city, but never the
> face of a friend,
> Till my heart grows sick with longing
> and dazed with the din of the
> street,
> As I listen to thronging thousands in a
> loneliness complete.

Do we, do I, treat Christ our Lord, as did those
frivolous people during the summertime? Christ
is God and therefore happy beyond the touch of
pilfering hands, but if His Manhood were not
united to the Godhead, would it not be grieved
beyond the healing at the unkindliness of men?
Could He not say with a truthfulness not known
to him who sang it: "A lonely man, oppressed
with lonely ills. . . . From all men's care, how
miserably apart!" He, who came from Heaven
for the sole purpose of making all men happy, is
the only one about whom we seem to care not at
all how lonely He may be. That visit to earth
cost Him His mortal life and we will not return
the call that sheer decency requires!

It takes time and it would spoil our pleasant
hours! What a strange commentary on a friend's
companionship! Will it cloud a summer's sky or
heighten the winter's cold to stop and have a chat
with the Lord and God of all? Will a few moments
spent with Him, who is to be our joy "while ages
course along," taint and tarnish our holidays or
load an extra burden on our shoulders? If it will,

the fault is not with Christ but with ourselves or with the companions we meet or the kind of holiday or work we engage in, and thus a piece of thoughtfulness on His part were He to spoil ahead of time that which would spoil our souls.

ॐ

Jesus, a strange sort of friend am I, yet a friend I still wish to be called. I hardly ever come to see You and pass by Your door as though I did not know who resides there. It must not happen again, yet it will without Your grace. So give, dear Lord, and give again and again that grace that will make me know and love and visit You.

COMFORT TO FRIENDS

May those who fear you rally to me, all those familiar with your decrees!
PSALMS 119:79

One of the surest spurs to renewed activity when we find our courage waning is the realization that we shall be a "credit" to those who love us and expect a great deal from us. The mere thought of all the hopes that friends have held in their hearts these many years and the joy that will come to them if we succeed in the allotted task makes our slackening will grow firm again and feeds new daring into a heart that would otherwise give up the fighting. It was thus when we were children, as we thought of the love that would glow in our mother's eyes and the praise that would come from our father's lips. And it is thus now, for in our older years it is still the thought of friends that urges us on anew.

Do we use similar thoughts to urge us on in the spiritual life? When my life is overcast by shadows that grow alarmingly darker and when my days are brightened by a sunlight that no clouds affect, is it the thought of the hopes of our Lord and of His earthly friends concerning me that teaches me to read my sorrows and my gladness correctly? It may be that I am torn away from every task to which my heart has ever had a native attachment and I find it hard to make the sacrifice of the dreams of years. It may be that while the lips of others move with laughter, my own are sharply closed with pain, that while other feet go straying where they will my own are pinioned helplessly. Do we then think that we must prove a credit to our changeless Friend and give joy to His friends to see us tried and proven, to find us loyal followers of a thorn-crowned King, who count no costs where there is a chance to follow Him more closely?

Again, when every shadow is gone and all life is full of such happiness as lies nearest to our desires and our heart is rich in all joys that earth can give, are we very careful not to be mismanaged by these passing exaltations but to take them with a humility and with a lowly mien so that all Christ's friends may be quite gladdened that we have learned from Him to be meek and humble of heart? On dark days and on bright, in the morning and at noon and in the evening of life, within my heart I must ever echo those inspiring words: "They that fear Thee shall see me, and shall be glad, because I have greatly hoped in Thy words," hoped in the time of soul-silence and desolation, when the voice of my Friend seemed hushed; hoped amid the noise of strongest pleasure when His voice was all but drowned by the noise of raucous creatures; hoped, too, on through colorless days when existence itself was most drab.

చిత

Jesus, my God, am I now a disappointment to You? As I look over my life, I feel I read the answer clearly written there, for despite the protestations I have made of my love, my deeds lack much of that holiness You would find in them. I fear I do but little credit to Your service and can scarcely be numbered among Your holy people. And so, dear Lord, it means You must be very lavish with Your grace so that I may no longer bring discredit to Your sacred name.

MAKING PEOPLE GRATEFUL

What could I have done for my vineyard that I have not done?

ISAIAH 5:4

"It takes an awful lot to make some people grateful," the high official said angrily when the people of a certain nation did not seem properly mindful of all the help that had been given them. Aid had come day after day and night after night. Neither money nor men had been spared and all the engines of modern commercial resourcefulness had been employed. Yet, after it all, there was only scant gratitude in return.

"It takes an awful lot to make some people grateful." Those words must often be on the lips of our Lord as He looks out from His home in the tabernacle! Long ago, when He was still visibly on this earth, He planned how best to help us. He saw our souls would be hungry for food that would make them strong and keep them pure, though the world was in league against us. And so He gave Himself to be our food, Himself, the strong "Lion of Juda," the spotless "Lamb of God." He saw that our hearts would long for a friend who would understand them, who would look down beneath all the foibles, beneath the sins of our lives, and see therein the deep craving for God that can be found tucked away somewhere in every human heart. And so He stayed with us as our changeless Friend and He abides with us by day and by night that we may come to Him when we like and as we like, with no constraint placed on our coming or our going, and tell Him all the joys and, much more, all the sorrows, of our lives.

Long before He took up residence with us, He swung the lanterns of the heavens for our coming and laid the foundations of the world for us. He stretched the earth's green carpet and cooled the air for us and watched carefully the admixture of its elements that it might support our frail breath of life. At His command, vegetable and animal life sprang into being for our sustenance, pleasure and amusement. Then, when all was done, He brought us, His children, into the home of His own building and bade us know and love and serve Him there.

Such love! Yet, as He gazes out upon us—or, if we cheat Him even of our visits, as He awaits a footfall that does not come—His Sacred Heart is lonely for our presence and much more lonely for our gratitude. If He had not done so much, this isolating forgetfulness of His cherished loved ones would not so cut His sensitive Heart.

ॐ

Dear Jesus, I, too, have been among those who have forgotten You. Indeed it does take "an awful lot to make some people grateful," and I am ashamed that, despite all You have done for me day after day, I have thanked You so very, very poorly. But, dear Jesus, this is in the past, and for it I humbly beg Your pardon. I shall do my best, dear Lord, in the days to come to show You by my frequent visits that I really do appreciate all You have done for me and I will be an ingrate no longer.

CONFIDANTS

My Beloved is mine and I am his. He pastures his flock among the lilies. Before the dawn-wind rises, before the shadows flee, return!

THE SONG OF SONGS 2:16, 17

My friend's complete confidence is what I long for. He may give me other gifts that indicate his love, but only let him grant me this,

the knowledge of himself, then I will be content
that I have found full favor in his eyes. To know
the projects that lie nearest his heart, to be asked
to give my own untempered views on all his
plans and aims and aspirations and to realize that
whatever he holds dearest is felt to be in surest
hands if it rests in mine, that is the finest gift he
can give me, the surest pledge of real affection.

We would have it the same with Christ, our
Friend. We know it is a bold desire, but who
would not be bold in loving such a friend? Others
have won it from Him. His mother Mary, of
course, knew His inmost heart, and by her right
as mother. Then there was John, "whom Jesus
loved," and lusty Peter and the world-encompass-
ing Paul. Again, a Catharine and a Teresa, a Bene-
dict, a Dominic, an Ignatius and even the boy
Stanislaus—they were confidants of Christ. And why
not we? But we are not saints.

If the price be that we must cast off ourselves
and put on the robes of sanctity, then we will
pay the price so that we may win our way to the
inmost recesses of the heart of Christ. All else is
paltry, worthless stuff and we should be abashed
to say that we had won such a priceless boon by
the forfeit of such things. We want to know, as
far as it is granted us, that He feels safe in trusting
us with His work, that He feels free in speaking
to us, as He did to His confidants of yore, of all
He plans to do within the souls of all. Yes, and
we will pay the price, by check on eye and ear
and tongue, that they may ever act as the eyes
and ears and tongue of Christ acted; yes, and
by unceasing guard over the portals of our hearts
so that no intruder may enter there, "for He
that would walk there would walk alone." Then,

when He has entered in and we have made Him much at home, we shall find true of Himself the words He spoke by Solomon long ago: "Behold He standeth behind our wall, looking through the windows, looking through the lattices. Behold my Beloved speaketh to me: 'Arise, make haste my love.' . . . My Beloved is mine and I am his. He pastures his flock among the lilies. Before the dawn-wind rises, before the shadows flee."

ह॰

Dear Jesus, I know as yet I cannot dare to ask that You treat me as Your confidant. So little of all my love has passed from word into fullness of work that I feel a proper hesitancy in asking for this favor. Still this I will beseech of You, that I may so improve, so grow to be Your "second self," that in the near future I may be one to whom You tell Your inmost secrets. Grant me this favor, dearest Lord, for it will mean that I shall love You more on this side of the grave, shall do Your work in better wise, and that our meeting in Heaven will be a deeper joy for all eternity to both of us.

THROWN RIGHT UP AGAINST GOD

Unload your burden on to Yahweh, and he will support you; he will never permit the virtuous to falter.

PSALMS 55:22

Well, thought the young man, here I am thrown right up against God! Great difficulties had come upon him, but one true friend had stood near him, comforting and helping him. Many of the trials were now gone, but not all. And now the friend must travel far away and the loneliness of it all bore in upon him. But the young man's faith cried out: "Well, here I am thrown right up against God!" And, kneeling down, he begged God for the grace to lean on Him alone.

"Thrown right up against God!" That is what often happens to most of us—with some, admittedly, more often than others. God may, indeed, grant us friends on whom we can lean and who can and do help us much in our times of stress and strain. For such friends we should thank Him, and use them, as He would have us use them, as supports to bring us through all trials and nearer and nearer to Him.

But such friends are not always near, and for some they are near only rarely. Then what? "Thrown right up against God!" Though all else be far away, He is always near; He can never be far away. He may *seem* far, far away, but that is only a temptation we must thrust from us. "Can a woman forget the child of her womb? And, even if she did forget, yet will I not forget Thee." Any thought of God's farness from us is only our vain, depressed imagining.

And it is very good to be so "thrown right up against God." It makes us realize our own insufficiency and the utter futility of getting lasting help from our fellowmen. They can aid us, of course, but only a little, and only for a time. The deeper, broader trials of life are too big for their helping.

And our own strength? It is in such hours of loneliness that we realize just what we are. Some days we seem quite big and brave and capable of solving all life's problems. But then the next day comes and all our valor is gone. Search our souls as we may, we can find no strength. Then it is we come to the stark realization that only in God can we find the ever-present Friend we need, powerful to help and kindly to heal, buttressing our soul with His graces.

ళం

Dear Lord, I need You as only a creature can need God. For the friends that You have given me I thank You and for my own strength, too. But those fail at times and must finally fail, for as Your handiwork, Your creature, I need *You*. It is, though, hard at times to come to You, to call upon You, to feel that You can and will help. So give me the grace always to have perfect confidence in You, above all then, when I am "thrown right up against God."

MISPLACED CONFIDENCE

Do your work before the appointed time and He in His time will give you your reward.

ECCLESIASTICUS 51:38

"We're through with you. You can't be trusted," the employer said to the young man.

He had shown promise and had made those who knew him feel that much could be placed in his hands. He had entered the office highly recommended, but now, after several months he was leaving and there was no one to raise a voice to help him. They could not. He had been trusted much and many responsibilities had been placed upon his shoulders. But those shoulders had sagged and refused to grapple with the problems and so across his life it is now written that no trust can be reposed in him.

When something like this happens to us, whether in large or small things, we feel a deep chagrin. It means we are worthless in men's eyes. But what would it be if God Himself were to tell us that we had proved unworthy of our trust? Death has come and all our years are examined for evidence of work well done. Far in the past we received our soul from God. It was a sacred trust. God placed His highest confidence in us and now, when life is over, what horror it is to hear from Him who cannot deceive or be deceived those damning words:

> Fresh and clean and immortal you received your souls from Me, and now you bring it back a tawdry, smirched and stunted thing. I gave you a real work to do, but My confidence was misplaced in you. You have received your soul in vain.

છે

Dear Jesus, by the love You have for me, never let me hear those awful words. You have placed a great deal of trust in me and I must measure up to it. Yet, there are times when I am shiftless and the responsibility of caring for my immortal soul grows irksome to me. Do save me from my laziness. Grant me the grace to work my work before the time, to shoulder life's duties and to trace out its problems so that, when You come to judge the living and the dead, I shall not be found to have received my soul in vain.

WITHOUT CHRIST— A FAILURE

Master, Simon replied, we worked hard all night long and caught nothing.

LUKE 5:5

It was early morning on the Galilean lake and the hills of Perea were still dominant against the sky. All through the night busy crafts had worked the inland sea and now weary men were guiding their boats to the welcoming shore. But one rode high upon the waters. Through the long hours its crew had swept the depths of the sea but had labored in vain. "We worked hard all night long and caught nothing."

There is nothing in life men want more than success, whether it is in the professions, the way of the tradesman or in other walks of life. Failure is the one thing that is dreaded, the one shadow that will darken each hour of life. To have labored as best we could, to have used up all our strength, to have planned with our eyes on yesterday and on tomorrow, and then to find that our life is only ashes is the deepest discouragement man can know.

If this is the story of our passing years, what then of the one supreme effort of life itself? What if it is a failure? To go to the grave without the goods of this world may be a grievous lot, but to go beyond the grave with nothing of the things of God to show, that means disaster for eternity. We are here to use the fleeting hours to gain new riches that neither time nor eternity can take from us so that when the summons comes that the Father wishes us we may hasten unto Him with laden arms. But is that the way we are laboring? God grant there be no mortal sin upon our souls, for that would mean that we were poor indeed and void of all that counts in terms of Heaven. But are we "jealous for the better gifts," ever alert to enrich our store of God's gift of sanctifying grace? This search for the gold of eternity should begin with our waking moments and sleep itself should be made to yield its measure of merit by being consecrated to God. An act of self-repression here, a passing deed that brings back a bit of joy to saddened hearts, the lifting of our own and other eyes to catch a clearer view of the farther shore —all these quite simple acts will leave us richer than we were. A hurried visit to our dearest Friend, a following of His footsteps when the steepness of the way would turn us back or the quick unyielding thrust that sends temptation far from us—these and their like will make us goodly in the sight of God.

৪৯

Dear Lord, as I kneel and think about my past I find myself so poor in all that counts for Heaven. I am so eager to chase after the things of the world, so slack in terms of working for what You died to purchase back for me. From this moment, dear Lord, may I cast aside my witlessness, learn to make my work, my play, my prayer, my every act, bring me nearer home with my hands filled with the graces of Your kindly giving.

LOVE TO THE END

Know that I am with you always; yes, to the end of time.

MATTHEW 28:20

Eternity will soon overtake each one of us. The sands of life are fast running out and most of us will soon come to the moment when the Lord comes to us to take a reckoning of our stewardship. For those who have been worldly, it is an hour of fear and foreboding, for they must then meet One who has stood in their midst and whom they have not known. They have not met our Lord before and there will be no friendly introduction, only the sentence of the Judge.

But to us, as the years pass rapidly by, that hour grows ever sweeter. We have loved the best Friend man has ever had. We have known "the beauty of His house and the place where His glory dwelleth." So, when we sit and prayerfully ponder over the years, we see to our comfort and joy the days and nights of the past gently darkened by the shadow of One with whom it has been our joy to tarry in sunshine and in rain. There was joy and the Friend of the bridegroom of Cana touched that joy and made it a sacred thing. We heard the cheering promise that He would be with us unto the consummation of the world and we have found Him so, true to His word. Other friends may come and go, may show us love that waxes and wanes like a fickle moon, but our constant, changeless Friend was with us all the time, ever the same in His kindness, ever the same in His love. Thus it has been and thus it will ever be. Even in the shadow of the grave our Friend is there. Loving His own, He loves us to the end and, as the shadows fall, He clasps more firmly His children's hands and leads us home through the dusk.

ॐ

O Jesus, sweet Friend, it is hard to see my life running on toward the end, hard to know my youth is gone and my mature years are passing. Hard, yes, Lord Jesus, very hard, unless I realize that each day that brings me nearer to the grave also brings me nearer to You. Home to You! How that drives the shadows back! O grave, where is thy victory? O death, where is thy sting, if the Lord of all, my Friend, is at my side to see me safely home? Dear Jesus, I trust You for my journey home. Speed me in my coming!

RESTLESS FOR GOD

It is he who made the Pleiades and Orion, who turns the dusk to dawn and day to darkest night. He summons the waters of the sea and pours them over the land. Yahweh is his name.

AMOS 5:8

There is a restlessness about our hearts that at times puzzles us. It is not merely our whims and moods but something deeper, a fundamental unrest that has caused the wisest of men to give it thought. Why is it thus, when the world holds out so much that is good and beautiful and true? Why is it that the heart of man must always seek and that, too, in a world where he is undoubtedly the proper tenant? Why is it that there is this hunger in our souls? Riches are sought and sometimes found, but peace does not come with them. Although honor may be ours, it brings with it a weight to our restive spirit. The pleasures of sense carry with them the seeds of a rude awakening. Are we, then, merely the playthings of the viler creatures that surround us?

No! The light of reason and the light of faith both show us so. There is a goal to our desires—but not where we are inclined to place it, not this side of the grave. Our hearts are small, but nothing can fill them save almighty God. Our desires may be classed and numbered by learned men, but nothing can adequately stay them except the limitless goodness of an infinite God. When we realize this, when we become intimately, completely conscious that the previously blind gropings of our hearts are instinctive strivings after God, what a chance we have of bringing down a magnificent unity into our lives! God for me, and I for God, everywhere, every time, always!

To give a speedier fulfillment to our hearts' deepest yearnings, to bring a quicker hush to their unrest, Jesus Christ, Son of the living God and living God Himself, is with us always and will be with us till He comes to judge the living and the dead. Generations pass and our Lord is always near in order that those who seek may find, in order that the long quest of our hearts may have its goal.

ॐ

Jesus, my God, my heart is so hard for me to understand. It seems "a strange, piteous, futile thing" and yet I know it was made for You and none but You can satisfy its craving. Yet here it seeks rest and there it seeks comfort, where none that lasts can be had. Teach me the vanity of human wishes, teach me that "the great show of this world is passing by," teach me and have me make the lesson live in my every act, that You and You alone are my heart's desire.

THE PLEASANTEST OF TASKS

Come and listen, all you who fear God, while I tell you what he has done for me.
PSALMS 66:16

The Greek philosopher Socrates was dead and his sorrowing disciples were clustered together talking about him. Each trait, each incident in his career, was recalled. They turned to Phaedo, his companion in his last hours, and asked that he tell them once more of the master's end. "Yes, I have the time and I shall try to tell you all," he said. "For indeed to recall Socrates, whether speaking himself or listening to another, is to me, at least, always the pleasantest of tasks."

Isn't this the story of all friends? Isn't it always "the pleasantest of tasks" to tell of a constant friend who has been with us in good times and bad, on whom we have leaned heavily at times and at others have walked by his side with a song on our lips, a friend from whom we have concealed nothing and who has revealed all his secrets to us? It was at those times when the hours passed most quickly and our hearts beat the fastest, when we spoke of dearest friends.

But there does seem to be an exception to this rule. There is one friend of whom many seem to hesitate to talk, one friend whose friendship some seem to want to hide. Some of us are quite abashed to be found in love with Christ. We hide our prayers lest we should be caught chatting with Him. We steal into His church with questioning eyes, lest others might detect us. We while away the hours with earthly friends, yet His name is scarcely mentioned or, if so, almost with an apology. But why? Is there any fault or blemish in Christ that we should hang our heads shamefully? Does it tarnish our honor to have His friendship? How strange we are! Christ is God with all God's boundless perfections, and He is Man, the highest, holiest, noblest man that has ever graced our world. Men may know from the facts of our lives that we consider Him our King and God, but in our daily behavior do we fear to let them see that we have a loyal Lover to whom our lives are pledged and whom we mean to please in all our ways? It ought to be sweet beyond the power of words for us to tell of the ways of our Friend, for us to let men know that it is our one ambition to be like Him in every thought, word and deed.

O Jesus, lover of my soul, You never were ashamed of having poor sinful me as the object of Your love. And yet at times, for fear of men's opinions, I find myself almost abashed to be known to be in love with You. Jesus dear, I will not have it so. I love You as I love none other. I hold You dear as I hold none other, and men shall know my love.

A LOVER'S WAY

I live now not with my own life but with the life of Christ who lives in me.
GALATIANS 2:20

It was a lonely grave, and at the grave a lone man wept as only men can weep. He was not a weakling, but within the earth lay the love of his young heart's choosing. "My heart is buried there," he repeated again and again, and his heart seemed empty.

So loved Abraham Lincoln. So love all true lovers. Love means the division of self, the sharing of our heart until it resides elsewhere than within our own small selves. That is what the pang of separation means, this pitiless plucking away and out of life of our other self.

Is Christ thus another self to us? We have been long years together and has He really grown to be —and we say it respectfully—"the other portion of our souls"? We trust He has. He is so real to us, so companionable, that were all other friends to fail or die, He alone would make our progress a happy journey home. He was with us in the days of childhood joy and as we passed into youth. He set His feet beside our own, lest they should stray. As the world and its problems invited us and we saw that youth must be done with forever, He stood by our side and held fast to our hands in order that the unfolding riddles of life might not numb our timid hearts. To Him we turn in our joy, to Him we go when we are frightened. Our other self? We trust so—yes, and more. Our only self, for to us life means Christ and we would like to be utterly one with Him, even to the day "when the shadow-valley opens, unlighted and unknown." That will be our final traveling; then He will welcome us to our Father's home. If He were gone, quite gone forever from our lives, we should kneel before the emptied tabernacle, as Lincoln at the grave, as Magdalene at the tomb, and cry unto the fruitless easing of our hearts. The life of our life would be gone!

૨☙

Jesus, the only Friend we need not fear to lose unless it be by willful truancy to love, be more and more to me each day I travel homeward. Make me lose self and selfish aims and think quite always of You alone, for that is the way of lovers and, poor as my heart may be, I long to be the best of all Your lovers. And yet a word, dear Jesus, more, for I must thank You from my deepest heart that You have pledged Your sacred presence with me to the end of days, and You alone know what that means to frail and timid me.

THE UNKNOWN GOD

I noticed, as I strolled around admiring your sacred monuments, that you had an altar inscribed: To An Unknown God.
ACTS 17:23

Dear Lord Jesus, how truly these words may be applied to our own altars! These altars of our numerous stately churches, these altars around which cluster the cottages of the straggling village—are they not all built to "an unknown God"? You are not known, my Jesus; else how explain the ways of men?

Your justice is unknown, else man would not sin. Your mercy is unknown, else the despondent sinner would not tarry in his guilt. Your patience, Your kindness, are not known, for if they were, would we play into the hands of the enemy by discouragement and irritation at our all too slight progress in perfection? Oh, we do not know You. You have been long with us, have tarried often in our hearts, and yet You are unknown. Your infinite love for us, Your infinite sympathy for us in all our trials, is unknown, it so far surpasses all we can imagine. "Lord Jesus, make me know You," know the great desires of your Sacred Heart, know the inspiring secrets of your life, that I may follow You unto perfection. Make me know You so that my love for You may be a living, real love for a living, real person. Be not almost two thousand years away from me, but be vividly, intimately, feelingly present for me. And when You come into my heart at the hour of Holy Communion, be not unknown to me. Take away the incognito of Your sacramental presence. Remove the veil that hides You from my earthly eyes and in the lineaments of Your sacred humanity speak unto me "as a friend would speak unto a friend." Then, Lord Jesus, I'll learn to make Your house my home, learn to come to You when the friction of mortal life wears deepest, learn to come to You and in Your sacred presence to enjoy a slight foretaste of the long bright day of eternity when I shall be safe at home with You.

TUCKING TROUBLES AWAY

Do not be like a lion at home, or a coward before your servants.

ECCLESIASTICUS 4:35

"Don't go near him now, he's in a bad humor." The word was passed about the office, then again throughout his home. It contained a bit of chiding and a good deal of fault-finding. At best, all that could be expected of him on that particular day was incivility. And so everyone —servants, clerks, friends, wife and children—all avoided him, leaving him to the isolation of his churlish ways. Lacking self-control, he was inclined to make his distemper of soul or body a cross for all about him.

Is there anything of the same sort in me? If my friends hear these words, would they think at once of me? If they would, it would be prudent and very Christian of me to understand my life correctly and mend my ways so that others, already bearing their own crosses, will not be forced to bear mine also. A headache comes and my temples throb, but is it right, just because *my* nerves are distraught, that I should set my neighbor's nerves to tingling? Sickness assails me and I am unable to help myself, but should I then make life simply drudgery for those who have to deal with me? My own life would be far sweeter and joy would be more consistently the lot of my family and friends were I to take my cross and accept it lovingly and then hide it away in my heart. At work, in the office, in the classroom, it is the weak, the immature, the uncontrolled, who make their attitude of mind, their views, their decisions and their approachableness depend upon a passing pain or trifling disappointment.

But it is hard to get an iron grip upon yourself! Whoever said otherwise didn't know of what he was speaking. "But can you smile with darkened mind and pain of heart and nerves stretched wide in agony?" Of course you can, but only when you have sought the Man of Sorrow and kept His company long and breathed in His broadened views of life and caught the contagion of His will.

ã€€ã€€ã€€ã€€ã€€ã€€ã€€à¸¿à¹…

Dear Jesus, I fear that I do not bear my crosses in the way I should. Long years ago I should have learned to smile when in fact I felt pain, to speak a kindly word when my temper was ill, to be affable when rudeness seems the way to ease my nerves. And yet I find these traits are so absent from my life! For the sake of my dignity as man, and much more for the sake of my higher calling to be another Christ, grant me plentiful grace to

carry all my crosses hidden away within myself
and all my troubles tucked away from sight.

BORROWING FUN

*I exult for joy in Yahweh, my soul rejoices
in my God.*

ISAIAH 61:10

"There's not much fun in it, unless you
do it for God," said the Venerable Philippine
Duchesne of her nine weeks' travel across the
ocean. At the time, the nineteenth century was
still young and the ships that crossed the ocean
were sorry things. Despite that, she had set out to
turn the hearts of the Indians toward Heaven. At
one moment there was a calm that held them
still upon the waves, at another a storm tossed
them across the billowing waves. Pirates gave
chase and sick men in the ship's narrow hold
breathed death into an atmosphere already heavy
with unendurable heat. Yet, to Mother Duchesne
and her followers there was fun in it because
they were doing it for God.

All of us complain at times that life is colorless. Our hearts are attuned to high romance and
our minds stray toward castles in the air. We find
it hard to see existence in the right way and to
catch the smile hidden in the open places of the
day. Yet catch it we must. But how? By bringing
God right down into our lives and playing the
hard, gruelling game of life with Him and for
His sake. Then there will be lots of fun in it, for
we would be seeing it through with Him, who

is our infinitely happy God. Mother at home "will start an Angel's wing" when she calls her little ones at dawn, sends them off to school and gathers them by her side as they kneel and say goodnight to God. Men and women in business will record deeds well done and temptations spurned indignantly. Teachers, too, will smile, as their Teacher-Master did centuries ago, when children crowded round Him, though the task be hard at times to mold young hearts to know and cling to Him with all the love their growing lives can find. No matter where we are, no matter what our work may be, the richness of God's smile will bring merriment into our life and set our hearts throbbing and put fun where only monotony reigned before.

ॐ

Jesus, dear, there is a lot of fun in life when You are present and I am conscious of Your presence. But when I forget You and try to play the game of life according to my own ways and rules, how blank and dull it becomes! My heart soon tires of it and keeps calling for a change and for new work and new scenes. Stay with me always and let me catch Your smile when You are pleased with me. Let me look within the shell of things and be conscious always of the deep abiding realities of my life and what a happy, joyous thing it is to see it through for You! Just teach me the fun of doing things for God!

A FRIEND IN NEED

So I say to you: Ask, and it will be given to you; search, and you will find; knock, and the door will be opened to you. For the one who asks always receives; the one who searches always finds; the one who knocks will always have the door opened to him.
LUKE 11:9, 10

In our hours of sorrow and darkness, there is nothing we dread so much as a rebuff or the slightest manifestation of inconsiderateness. Our souls swiftly recoil before the slightest touch of harshness, fearful of another bruise, dreading another cross. That is why, when joy's sunlight has departed from our lives and there are shadows across our paths, we turn our groping steps away from those that know us least and love us little, turn them away to search out one who understands us well and who will lay none but the gentlest hands on our hearts. We seek a friend who knows our strength and our weakness too, who knows our faults of character and whatever virtues may offset them, and thus knows how to shift the burden so that we may bear it best. But if there be no shifting of the weight, then with friend's true skill he will recall in vivid freshness the motives that quicken us best and spur us most instantly into action and we shall rise again and find our burden lighter because our hearts are brave, as they were of old, and young with a youth we had thought forever lost.

It is a blessed thing to find such friends and

we should grapple them to us with hooks of steel.
Yet there are men and women whose solitude of
sorrow is never broken by a cheering word, who
listen to the feet that hurry by and sickeningly
know that none will ever turn aside to seek them
out. There are others whose friends are kind
for the hours when there is laughter but miserly
of even a word of pity when the smile is gone.
Still others—and perhaps God has seen fit at times
to have us numbered among them—whose hearts
are so sorely harassed and whose shoulders are
so bowed by mortal cares that no human touch,
however gentle and kind, can bring them comfort
in their woe.

The deep, strong consolation in these lonely
hours is to come to the "Man, Christ Jesus," to
come to Him in His hiding behind the sacramental veils. To Him we may tell the tale He
knows so well, but which He will never tire of
hearing from us, so that our hearts may be eased
thereby. His house is the house of prayer, the
home of all supplication, the place where the
sick and the halt and the blind of soul and of
body come when the shadows fall, to meet their
Divine Friend who never once has crushed the
bruised reed nor quenched the burning flax. There
the most poignant of human woes, there the most
secret sorrows of human life, may be whispered and
ever will fresh hope and strength arise within us, as
Jesus, the Man of Sorrows, who trod the wine-press
alone, cheers and consoles us in our faintness. There
is nothing that we can plead for that He cannot
give, nothing we can ask for that He will not bestow
if only it be for our good. Give, He always does,
whether it be the object of our own poor prayers or
a grace He sees more fitted to our needs. Then,

when we kneel before Him, there is courage in our souls "to strive, seek, to find and not to yield."

છે

Jesus, friend of the weary and faint of heart, who can tell what You are to us in hours of loneliness and grief? Life has its joys and we thank You from our hearts for them, for those brief foretastes as they are of eternal bliss. But life has its sorrows, too, sorrows so often unsharable and unshared. To You, then, we come and lay before You the wounds we have received. Jesus, You will help us bear them, You will listen to our oft-told tale, will You not, dear Lord? If you do, will not the joy be Yours, as well as ours, when we, whom You have saved, meet You on the farther shore?

WHEN I'M THROUGH, I'M THROUGH

Forgive us our debts, as we have forgiven those who are in debt to us.
MATTHEW 6:12

She was a willful and petulant young lady who had just had a falling-out with her best friend and the right was only slightly on her own side. Stubbornly, she kept insisting: "When I'm through, I'm through." "Well, all right," said her friend in a final attempt to bring her back to reason, "suppose God said that to you? You've offended Him. What if He said: 'When I'm through, I'm through'?"

Our Lord knew human nature and how hard we find it to forgive. He knew how hearts rankle and how brooding over offenses makes them worse and heightens them beyond all recognition. And so it was that into the one prayer He taught us He put those words that cut right into the heart of common human fault: "Forgive us our trespasses as we forgive those who trespass against us." He makes us ask that the measure of God's forgiveness to us will be exactly the measure of our forgiveness of others. He makes us "take our own medicine."

There may, of course, be times when I might legitimately deny, not forgiveness—no, never—but a renewal of close intimacy. No one can claim my friendship anew when he or she has seriously violated it. My friendship is something I may give or withhold and none can demand it of me. Christ Himself was not a "friend" to each and every man He met; He was a "friend" to His chosen disciples. He certainly was no "friend" of the Pharisees and Sadducees.

But forgiveness is another thing, and Christ has told us that we must forgive not seven times but seventy times seven times. And how many of us are ever offended even in the longest life that often by any one friend?

"Forgive and forget" is a wise piece of advice and it makes life much happier if we follow it. What a silly thing it is to retain some trifling offense against another! Do I like it if someone does the same against me for some small slip that I never meant? And even when I meant it and was sorry afterward, didn't I expect them to be "reasonable" and forgive? There is a very old saying: "Do as you would be done by." Life is hard at best, without making it harder for everyone by silly unforgiveness. And is it not generally best to mend a friendship when it has been strained? Isn't everyone happier?

ॐ

Dear Jesus, You touched the sore spot of our human littleness when You taught us to pray as You did. You know how petty and mean and small we are and how prone we are to "hold things in." It is a mean trait and we hate to have others act in the same way toward us. I say the prayer You taught me often each day and I cannot say it honestly unless I forgive and forget. And I do want to say it honestly.

A FRIEND'S MEANNESS

Even my closest and most trusted friend, who shared my table, rebels against me.
PSALMS 41:9

Even in the closest of human friendships, there is a point of tension beyond which there is sharp cleavage. The unwarrantable repetition of the same offense or the willful accumulation of varied insults and injuries at last costs us the love of our friend, and rightly so. The least that is expected from friends is some little return of love, and so when all show of affection has ceased and in its stead ungrateful discourtesies abound, then a parting comes and reunion is denied forever.

This we know well of purely human friendship and is it not often why we are prudently thoughtful not to try our friend too keenly? For, though his love be deep, it is at best a limited love of a created being. This wholesome restraint seems not to be present in our relations with our Lord. I know it is a grievous thing to offend the God who made me, the Saviour who died for me and the Friend who is ever present on the altar to be the food and life of my soul. I know it is traitorous to forswear my changeless Friend in any least way, and yet what of my life? Am I really as careful to avoid what displeases Him as I am to leave undone that which would irritate an earthly friend? When I chat with Him in prayer, do I not often rudely break the conversation off and pay no attention to my Guest? I have an appointment with Him every morning and evening, to greet Him as the day breaks and when it wanes and again each Sunday morning to come to His home to be with Him, when He once more offers Himself in sacrifice for the sins of man. Do I, with proper politeness, keep that appointment and come with promptness?

I have a pressing, very urgent, invitation from the same Lord to come and break my fast with Him each day, to feed my soul on His nourishing flesh and blood. Yet time and again I have spurned the invitation and other times come and acted quite rudely. Yes, at times I have so tired of His company that I shortened the time of entertaining Him and rudely lessened the moments of thanksgiving after Communion. Then, in all the other ways do I show a decent respect for my Friend's feelings? Can it really be just because I know His patience will never be exhausted that

I find myself so discourteous? Is the very goodness of my Friend to be cruelly used as a means to injure His sensitiveness? For, indeed, our Lord is very sensitive and feels our slights and petty meannesses more than any earthly friend could ever feel them.

ॐ

Jesus, was ever anyone as rude and boorish as I? The story of our friendship is a story that would make a decent man hang his head in shame and yet I seem to lack all shame. I speak loudly of my love for You and yet I do not hesitate to cause You pain, whenever and wherever I so choose. I tell men You are my best Friend and then when we are alone—and sometimes even before others—I start again to play my insulting part. Oh, dear Jesus, it looks all too black, and yet You must forgive me. It is all a shameful lack of courtesy, sheer impudence, that an earthly friend would never tolerate. But have mercy on me now, and forgive me all, and I shall strive to act more decently hereafter.

SEEING BUT NOT ENTERING IN

You may see this land only from afar; you cannot enter it, this land that I am giving to the sons of Israel.

DEUTERONOMY 32:52

"What's the use of trying hard and playing straight?" said the man who felt he'd been double-crossed. "I worked hard and didn't think of myself. I lost sight of my personal aims in order that the work assigned might go well. And look what happened! I was kicked out on the street!" It was one of life's tragedies: a man cheated of his well-deserved reward, a man who had played straight in the game of life but found the dice were loaded. And the man he was speaking to re- alized that his embittered soul must be handled gently, lest the hurt mar him irrevocably.

Life, indeed, has many disappointments and trials and it is hard to measure one against the other for they all hurt so much and hurt in vari- ous ways. Yet surely it is a searching trial that shakes strong men when, at the peak of success or just as long-laid plans are maturing, they are severed rudely and definitely from their work. It may be the chance give-and-take of life or, harder still, a misunderstanding, or, hardest yet, jealousy, which has thrown the switch that caused the wreckage. And it is hard to see others come and reap the harvest that has been sown and care- fully nurtured. They stand before the world and win its praise. And what of the other? No man ever thinks of him, of the man who did the work, or pays the smallest tribute to his labors.

Such a trial may come to all of us, and it would be well for us to study our soul when it does come. It may be parents who have labored, as parents do, for many years and stinted themselves in many things in order that their child might profit and achieve more of life's goods than they. Then the child grows up and the mother and father are often forgotten, or worse still, snubbed. The child reaps now, where it has not sown.

A teacher toils in school and after school does

much with the young people to push back the borders of ignorance and to bring healthy discipline into their lives. And then another, more assertive or more ingratiating, gets the credit for it all and the one who did the drudgery is passed by. It's not an easy dose to take and it needs a fully mature will to stand by silently and show no lack of manners.

It is the same in the world of business and in public service and private helpfulness. It is not easy to exert the self-control required when one has given much of self and then seen another reap the glory.

Such is life, time and time again. The trial is a hard one, but it means everything in those hours of trial to be fully conscious that we have done all for God. If, in all truthfulness, I can say that the one thing I sought was to do God's will and further His glory, then, indeed, will my cross be lightened; then, indeed, will I reap where none can steal from me. I did it all for God and He knows it. Why, then, bother with the praise of men, a praise that has been so well well described as a "dying echo"? Is anything more insubstantial than that? And if so insubstantial, is it worth seeking after?

ह्ल

Dear Jesus, I find it very hard when others get the praise that by every right should be my own. I know it is supremely foolish for me to care what men may think, but that is the way we creatures are made. You know my weakness and You must pity me for craving so incontinently for such a fitful, insubstantial thing. But the stark fact is: I do. So, help me, Lord, to be less foolish and to care only for the praise that comes from You.

LIFE'S UPS AND DOWNS

Yahweh will come and rest on the whole stretch of Mount Zion and on those who are gathered there, a cloud by day, and smoke, and by night the brightness of a flaring fire. For, over all, the glory of Yahweh will be a canopy and a tent to give shade by day from the heat, refuge and shelter from the storm and rain.

ISAIAH 4:5, 6

No man's life runs smoothly and unbrokenly. To us all in God's good time comes the constant interchange of light and darkness which perfects what we call our life. Sorrow comes and joy rides close behind it. Today, as we sit about, no darkness reigns in our home, but tomorrow the vacant chair tells again the world-old story. Life is a hard reality, at times a very hard reality, so hard that our hearts are frightened at the vision of our own cheated dreams. Childhood days pictured a fairyland world where "grown-ups" moved and were wondrously happy, the envied masters of themselves. But childhood days have faded into the misty past and with them their fairyland, and time has made life tell its own true changing story. Grief has long since burdened our faltering hearts: grief for those that are with us no more; grief for the living whose wayward lives make it hard to check the ever-rising prayer that God had deigned long since to call them to Himself; grief for our own sad mistakes that may mark too closely our waning days. But, then, as day drives back the night, joy, too, has come: the joy of well-merited success and the fullness of heart as we told our loved ones the long story of efforts crowned at last; the joy of father and mother as they watch their children growing into maturity, shielded from the world's dark shafts; the joy of holy men and women who have presented the sun with their cloistered rising to praise their God and labor all day in the classroom or at the bedside of the sick, teaching souls to love the God who made them.

Life has its sorrows and life has its joys, too, but its sorrows will be all too heavy and its joys will be tainted and unsanctified unless we bring them one and all to the foot of the altar. There is the "tabernacle for a shade in the daytime from the heat," the daytime of pleasure when all is well with us and we are prone to forget our God, and "for a security and covert from the whirlwind and from rain," and the darkness of trial and over-burdening grief. To us the Prophet Balaam speaks in ways beyond his knowing: "How beautiful are thy tabernacles, O Jacob, and thy tents, O Israel" —the tabernacles where Emmanuel dwells, the tents where the Son of Man lingers yet a while— "as woody valleys, as watered gardens near the rivers, as tabernacles which the Lord hath pitched, as cedars by the waterside!" There is our good Master, waiting for us in the dawnlight as He waited of old for Magdalene; listening for our footfall at His humble home in Galilee. He will be to us "a cloud by day, and smoke, and by night the brightness of a flaring fire," ever guiding, ever leading us on unwaveringly to our home beyond the grave.

၆၈

Jesus, gentle Saviour, God of wondrous fore-thought for those You love, life is all too strange a problem for me to face alone. I need You for my guide, that I fail not in the dark and wander not in the noonday of my powers. Be close to me, then, good Jesus, and leave me not alone. I know You do not, but what I mean is, make me know, make me remember, that You are with me always. When the sun of life shines full, make me mindful of You, the Man of Sorrows, "who having joy set before Him endured the Cross, despising the shame," and when the night of grief steals from us the light we love so much, let me remember that "this everyone is sure of that worshippeth Thee, that his life, if it be under trial, shall be crowned: and if it be under tribulation, it shall be delivered: and if it be under correction, it shall be allowed to come to mercy. For Thou are not delighted in our being lost, because after a storm Thou makest a calm and after tears and weeping Thou pourest in joyfulness.

DEAD DREAMS
IN THEIR EYES

After this, many of his disciples left him and stopped going with him.　　JOHN 6:66

There she sat—not insolent, not aggressive—just sat. "No," she said, "I don't even want to be helped. It's not that I intend to do wrong. I have done wrong, and if he recovers, probably will do wrong again. I don't know. But I just don't care either way any longer."

As he looked into her eyes, dead dreams looked out. There before him was a corpse. Not the corpse of a body, but the more terrifying soul-corpse from which life had fled. And the dead dreams in her eyes laid icy hands upon him.

The woman had had her dreams of womanly virtue. She had long held to them, from girlhood into maturity and on through the years. But her ideals had become tarnished, her companions had struck at them again and again, her teachers had sneered at them, and slowly the vision had faded and life was now a drab, dull thing which held out nothing.

Dead dreams in her eyes! And as he pondered how he might help her relight those dreams, his thoughts swept over the world and peered into the throngs of men.

Here were young people who were being trained in schools that ignored God. Men and women of older years had learned of God and His manifold goodness. But current philosophers had turned their minds from such thoughts and had taught them to fill their souls with the things of the time.

But sadder sights as well appeared before him. Within Christian homes and even within the sanctuary rail, gazed out eyes dimmed with fading and faded dreams. Christ had won their hearts when they were younger, had heard them pledge their love to Him, and Christ had blessed that

love and sealed it as His own. And then as the
years slowly passed and the friction of life bore
in upon them and the things of the world took
on fresh allure, Christ had seemed not so lovable
and His wishes not so worthwhile, and the vision
had begun to dim.

૭☙

Dear Jesus, You have been good enough to
teach me much of Your love and to win my love
in return. I know You are worthy of the best that
is in me and that, try as I may, I can never be
worthy of Your love or measure up to Your ideals.
But the world is loud in its clamors and the things
of the world beckon very appealingly, and at
times it is quite difficult to hold my heart from
truancy. But I do want to keep the vision bright
and I do want to love and serve You always. And
so, please never let there be in my eyes dead
dreams of You.

KEEPING THE PAST
IN MIND

*You must not molest the stranger or oppress
him, for you lived as strangers in the land
of Egypt.*

EXODUS 22:21

The Jews had fled from Egypt and were
now camped in the great plain at the foot of Sinai,
"the mountain of God." There, for eleven long
months, they were taught by God through Moses,

and today they are listening to solemn words that chide them unto justice and fair dealing. They are told to be mindful of their own hard past, of the days and the weeks and the months and the years of their own exiled labor and slavery in the land of the Pharaohs, so that when strangers come to them and ask sanctuary and succor from them they might be merciful and hearken to their prayers.

To remember our own sad and sinful past is to bring a steadying and maturing force into our lives. Not that we must see only the dark moments, for that would be unfair to self and hardly fair to the generosity of our Lord. Yet we must keep our failures well in sight and with healthy introspection view and review the times and reasons for our falls, so that we may not "molest a stranger or oppress him," since we ourselves also were "strangers in the land of Egypt."

If we recall the days when angry words escaped us and we lost the poise of character that befits all men and women, we shall have a bit of patience when another acts with the same lack of control. When others unthinkingly ride roughshod over our high-strung nerves, would it not be very helpful to go back into the past and recall how often we have unwittingly, wholly unintentionally, made other hearts bleed? Yes, and even if the pain be deliberately and willfully inflicted on us, may there not be at least a few occasions in the past when we, too, mercilessly found it within ourselves to cut and wound and take pleasure in making another exiled heart ache? Again, when we find others following low standards or ideals, our hearts are angered and we play the harsh censor—but not if we remember the days when we, too, gave up the quest of higher things and slackened in our zeal for the ways of sanctity. Prayers neglected or apparently ill-said will make us think of many a morning and evening when we were scant in our politeness to God. Petty deceits will bring up the picture of actions on our part that we would not have scrutinized too closely and ways quite selfish and self-centered will make us blush because of their striking likeness to the many, many acts wherein the "I" was all that could be seen.

ह॰

Jesus, dearest Lord, remember that years and years ago You said: "I am the Lord, thy healer." Heal me then, and cleanse me of all that is displeasing in Your sight. I learn so little from my past. I profit so scantily from experience. I know my own frailty and yet when I see a fellow-struggler fall, I am so prone to lift an accusing finger, so quick to raise a critical voice. Give me grace, then, I beg of You, plentiful grace so that I may always keep fresh the memory that I, too, have been "a stranger in the land of Egypt."

GOD MADE ME PURPOSELY

You ordered all things by measure, number, weight.

WISDOM 11:21

One of the major things to realize in life is that God had a set purpose in mind when He made *me*, that He had a definite idea what He wanted me to be and what He wanted me to do. That puts a special stamp on my life and gives a determination and a precision to my whole outlook.

I am not here by chance, a by-product of an evolution that is headed nowhere but just happens to be putting out new products of its own unending changefulness. I come definitely from somewhere—from God. I am headed definitely toward somewhere—toward God. In the meantime, I have something quite definite to do: something set by God.

My origin, my purpose, my work in life, is precisely what we mean by a vocation in life. Vocation means "calling," something to which God is inviting me. It may be that I have not yet been able to decide just what it is to which God is beckoning me. Then I must pray that I may hear His call clearly and hearken to it readily.

It may be that He calls me to married life, where I shall pledge my love and loyalty and receive in return a like pledged love and loyalty. Then will God want us both to seal that love within His love and guide our blended lives according to His law. Hand in hand He would have us walk Heavenward and make the way there a holy and happy one.

Or He may be calling me to give Him my undivided love and to serve within His cloistered walls. He will be a jealous lover and want all of my love. And in return? He will give me lavishly of His love and fill my soul with grace and give me a peace that the world does not know and cannot take away. Will my way be a lonely one? Yes, if one can be lonely with God.

Or, again, He might be asking me, through circumstances over which I have no control, to forego the happiness of marriage and yet to live in the world. Those at home may demand my time and care and support. Or sickness may prevent me from serving Him in the religious life. Then God is calling me definitely to serve Him. The sacrifice may be a very great one; but if I make it cheerfully and for Him and because He wants it, then I can reach great sanctity because I am cooperating with God's plans for me.

෫෩

Dear Jesus, I want to make of my life just what You want it to be. I want to serve You at all times, cheerfully and willingly and generously. In every place and under all circumstances I want to carry out Your plans. You made me purposely and I want to fulfill that purpose no matter what it is.

FALL IN LOVE WITH GOD

But you, my dear friends, must use your most holy faith as your foundation and build on that, praying in the Holy Spirit; keep yourselves within the love of God and wait for the mercy of our Lord Jesus Christ to give you eternal life.

JUDE 1:20, 21

"Well, the rooms are a little small, and I'm not too pleased with the neighborhood, but

Mary wants it and I guess it's all right." "Mary
wants it" was the thought that solved the problem
and made satisfactory things which otherwise
would have been distasteful. As Saint Augustine
said many hundreds of years ago: "Where there
is love, there is no toil; or if there is toil, the toil
is loved." So Bill was willing to overlook the
things he did not like because Mary wanted the
apartment. They were in love and planning their
first home.

Love makes all things easy. That is why we
would be very wise to fall desperately in love with
God. Life has many joys and happinesses, but life
has many shadows, too, and many crosses. None
of us finds it hard to accept life's joys, but we
need help to manage life's trials as we should. But
it is something we can do when we know God and
see His guiding hand in everything and love Him
above everything.

Differences inevitably arise between husband
and wife. Sooner or later the thrill of newly-won
love wears off and colorless years lie ahead. That
is when it is so easy for them to let things get
"messed up" if they think only of themselves
and their petty selfishness. But it is so easy, too,
to take the jolts of life with a smile and to
shoulder the crosses as they come if God's love
has remained lighted in their hearts.

Between friend and friend old joy wanes and
sharp clashes break in. It seems to be almost un-
avoidable. Yet, if both still love God, the dis-
agreement is soon forgotten and the friendship
is resumed.

The same holds true in my own individual
life. If life brings deteriorating health and pain
of body, none will see me straining at the leash,

for there will be little straining when once I
realize that God has sent me these crosses. If my
best-laid plans go awry and my castles in the air
dissolve, the fact that God has allowed these things
to happen makes me accept the frustrations readily. For He knows best—and I am in love with God.

If only we would really fall in love with God!
What a changed thing life would be! There are
times when His law seems so hard, when it seems
to cheat me of so much that I want, so much to
which I seem to have a right. That law binds me
here and checks me there. It often cramps my
style. Unless I love God and love Him with my
whole heart and soul. Half-love has never yet made
anything easy. But true love can make a squalid
neighborhood seem a garden. And, if love between man and woman can do that, what will
not the love between man and God do?

ào

Dear Jesus, even from a selfish standpoint I
ought to love You. But selfishness is quite an
unworthy motive. I want to love You for Your
own sake and because of all You are and all that
You have given me. Then, whether sun shines
or clouds gather, life will be filled with peace,
that peace of Yours which the world cannot give
and cannot take away. Dear Lord, grant that I
may fall in love with You.

AN EPIC OUT OF
TWO GRUNTS

What I command you is to love one another.
JOHN 15:17

The scene was a movie location and the filming was being held up because of a fight between two actors over which one would grunt the two grunts called for at that particular point. Suddenly the director appeared, sized up the situation and roared: "Don't make an epic out of two grunts!"

It was all very comic—and very stupid too. But it's the same thing that goes on a thousand times a day in our lives: at home, at school, in the office, in social affairs. The squabble over "two grunts" can bring much unhappiness and offset great good.

Some little thing goes wrong at home and, instead of overlooking it, father loses his temper. A child is troublesome at just the wrong time and mother gets into a rage that is quite uncalled for. A son or a daughter asks for some small permission that is denied and, forgetful of obedience, stages a scene. All could have been forgotten in a moment, but instead, the peace and the harmony of the home is lost for hours.

In the office, a clerk makes a trifling mistake and, instead of remembering that such mistakes are almost bound to happen, his superior places the poor man "on the carpet." It was a mistake, yes—but was it any bigger than the "two grunts" on the movie location? Or, perhaps, the boss is out of sorts and snaps out an order quite rudely and the clerks react by staging a slowdown in the work when they could in fact best handle the situation by a shrug of the shoulders and then forget about it.

It may be that a committee is formed of which I wanted to be chairman, but someone else has been selected instead. Or a teacher is named for a class that I hoped to get. Or I am not chosen for a part in a play upon which I had set my heart. It is easy, then, to pout and to get bitter. Any child can do that.

But is it all sensible? Will it make any difference a hundred years from now? Will it make the slightest ripple in the whirlpool of history? Will "generations yet unborn" read tearfully of the gross injustice done me?

And is it what our Lord would wish? Honestly, if He were present on the scene, am I sure that He would approve of my way of acting? Hardly. "My peace I leave you; My peace I give you"; "A new commandment I give unto you: that you love one another as I have loved you, that you also love one another"; "But I say to you, love your enemies; do good to them that hate you: and pray for them that persecute and calumniate you: that you may be the children of your Father who is in Heaven." His command was love, repeated, insisted upon and made the test of being His disciple. Surely He could never approve of making "an epic out of two grunts."

ဢ

Dear Jesus, give me a bit of common sense and, more than that, give me a bit of Your own poise. There are many things in life that bring irritation and friction. Others *are* thoughtless and inconsiderate at times, and even unjust. But I would be more mature and more of a Christian if I handled the upsets in a self-controlled way. It's all very clear to me now in the quiet of prayer, but it is not so clear at the moment when things are going wrong. And so I beg You now to give me then, and always, grace enough not to make "an epic out of two grunts."

LIVING OUR LESSONS

Now that is hardly the way you have learned from Christ.

EPHESIANS 4:20

Saint Paul is speaking to the Ephesians, warning them not to return to their former evil ways from which their conversion to Christ had won them. They are to "put off the old man," which meant all the evil ways of acting that they had learned as pagans: impurity, disobedience, hatred, quarreling, self-seeking and a complete surrender to a mad attempt to have all the pleasures of this world without any restraint. They had become Christians now and had "learned from Christ"—learned what He thought, what He desired, what He wanted them to do and what He wanted them to avoid. Living in a city that was notorious for its vice and rottenness, wherein temptations were ever present, Saint Paul warned them to be on their guard.

That warning is sound for us today. Ephesus

was filthy and the world of our time often follows it closely. In entertainment, in so-called sexual freedom, in the business world, the old standards have begun to disappear; politics and public life are rife with graft and scandal.

But we Christians have "learned from Christ." We know His law and His counsels: purity and modesty, honesty and truthfulness, self-restraint and self-control. All that is highest in life He stands for; all that is noblest, all that is truest. He does not seek to thwart our happiness, but He must insist that we be true to the basic demands of our nature. And, while He does not oblige us thereto, He does hold out to us the higher reaches of sanctity, to which the saints have climbed and to which He calls each willing soul.

Thus have we learned from Christ and thus should we show to the world the lessons we have learned.

ह्ल

Dear Jesus, I have not been a very apt student. I know well enough what You want me to do and how You want me to behave myself. I have learned the lessons of the head well enough, but not the lessons of the heart, which bring my life in line with what I know. I have followed the call of the world in many things when I know You would not approve, for I have not so learned from You. I am sorry for these failures; with Your grace I shall carry Your lessons out in my life better hereafter than I have in the past.

MY FRIEND'S FRIENDS

I tell you solemnly, in so far as you did this to one of the least of these brothers of mine, you did it to me.

MATTHEW 25:40

Criticism always shows lack of maturity. To sit in superior judgment on others, to define offhandedly the method of procedure in cases that have taxed many an older mind, to parade the defects and sins of others, is to show that we know human nature neither in general nor our own particular. But when the criticism is of my friend or of my friend's friends, then it is a bit of childishness, deeply tainted with the unseemliest of faults, untrueness to my friend.

It would be a good idea to think of this frequently. To criticize my fellowman, whoever he is, indicates that I am as yet in my youth, my immaturity. It brands me as unfaithful to friendship's finest trait, for all men are the friends of my own best friend, Christ Jesus. He has loved them all unto His dying on the Cross and loves them yet. He loves those who are smirched with sin and the blackest crimes and He reaches out to them. Others love Him fitfully, but despite their fickleness His love for them is unchanging. Still others love Him with undying, eager love and serve Him well. They, too, are His friends. There is no man alive who is not Christ's friend. It is, therefore, an act of sheer impoliteness for me to talk about my Friend's friends and that in His presence, too, since He is everywhere. There may be faults, even the grossest of crimes, in their lives, but shall I speak of them? Is it not enough for my Friend to know that men that He loves are spoiling His handiwork without my heralding the fact abroad? And, if His dearest friends, the saintly men and women about us, fail at times in little ways and do not fully measure up to the stature of Christ, shall I further pain my Friend by pointing a finger at their lack of love? All have their faults, as I have many of my own, and yet Christ, who knows them all and knows their frailties, still holds them as His friends. Friends they are of His and as His friends I must learn to think of them and speak of them and find no pleasure in telling of their waywardness.

ॐ

Again, dear Jesus, with You alone do I fail in friendship's least demands. Of those whom my earthly friends hold dear I never speak unkindly, yet of the souls You love I would tell the slightest faults, forgetful of Your sacred presence and the pain I cause You. Let this never happen again. Your friends must be my friends and, if they have their faults, I shall try to keep them hid. Yes, and if I can, lend a helping hand to make them grow more like You.

SAYING THANK YOU

Were not all ten made clean? The other nine, where are they?   LUKE 17:17

To say "thank you" is the minimum of politeness expected and required of all. To snatch a gift from the hands of the giver and to hasten away without even a hurried expression of thanks stamps one as an ingrate and such a person finds himself, sooner or later, shunned by all.

Tested by this standard, how many of us would be found to be gentlemen and ladies with our Lord? He would have all be polite with Him, but more especially those who lay special claim to His friendship. Yet, in the Book of Life, how often we have petitioned and how infrequently we have bothered to give thanks! It is a sad commentary on the choicest of friendships.

In our hours of trial we hasten to our Lord and plead with Him for all His love and call upon Him to free us from a chalice that is too bitter for our tasting and He hearkens to our plea. Do we think to thank Him for it when our health, grown poor, returns? Do we think to thank Him when we have been led out of the captivity of sin and back to the fullness of His love? Perhaps in the night of our soul we cry for light as we stumble along a narrow path, but when the light is given and we run joyfully along the way of perfection, we forget to be thankful for the brightness of the way and the music of our hearts. We forget—but suppose our Friend had forgotten to hear our cry!

What, too, of gratitude for the daily gifts of nature and of grace; for life and the wonderful powers of soul and body, the love of parents and of children and of friends; for the still more precious gifts of faith and grace, of the Church and of His consoling presence? Have we never a "Thank you, Lord" for all of these?

ॐ

Dear Lord, why is it I forget the niceties of friendship only with You? To all other friends I am grateful, but when You give a gift I snatch it with the swift eagerness of childhood and hurry away with no thought of the kindly Giver. But, Jesus, You know I am grateful, if it be with the gratitude of only a thoughtless, loving child. So pardon all my impoliteness and trust me, dearest Lord, for a better, more thankful future.

CHANGE THE SIGN

Anyone who does not carry his cross and come after me cannot be my disciple.
                                        LUKE 14:27

"Did you ever study algebra?" he asked. "Why, yes, but I don't see how that's going to help me in this trouble." "Well, maybe you don't, but here: this figure is 2. It can be +2 or −2. If it is 'plus 2,' it is a help; if it is 'minus 2,' it's a liability." "But again, what's that got to do with my trouble?" "Well, Jack, it has this much to do with it: God has sent you this cross of ill-health, which cheats you of your ambitions and irks you so much. That ill-health will be a liability to you if you get out of sorts and murmur and complain. But it will be an asset, something worth while, a positive help, if you accept it gracefully from God's hands. That means carrying your cross, not letting it knock you down."

"Change the sign: plus 2 or minus 2." Isn't

that the story of life? It's all in the sign, all in the way that we take the troubles that come to all of us.

Ill-health comes—and no one likes ill-health. I can balk at it and bend under it and become a burden to myself and to others. Or I can take it with a smile and bear my pain without a whimper and thus become a real consolation to those about me.

My best plans go awry and all my hopes deteriorate into ashes; defeat overcomes me and I become discouraged. I act like a spoiled child that can't have its way. But, if I master my disappointment and remain in control, then I am stronger and holier by the very reason of the defeat.

"Change the sign." There is nothing that happens to me in life that cannot be turned into asset or liability. Success can make me become proud or it can make me humble. Happiness can make me forget God or it can bring words of thanksgiving to my lips. Good health can make me too self-reliant or it can spur my efforts to be very close to God and to help as many others as I can.

~

Dear Jesus, help me to learn to "change the sign." Each and every thing that happens to me will either help or hinder me—and it is I who make the difference. At times it is really hard to make each cross or trial, and harder still at times to make each success or happiness, bring me nearer to You, because I am so weak and fickle. But Lord, by Your own examples You have shown me how to carry my cross in the right way and You always give me grace to handle the situation well. So I will try always to "change the sign."

HE IS ALWAYS
NEAR

*I will not leave you orphans; I will come
back to you.*

JOHN 14:18

Sometimes the isolation of the human
soul comes with a force that carries with it a realization that brings terror to us. Between my soul
and the souls around me there is a gulf so broad
and deep that all the powers of human expression
cannot span it. Then I need uplifting sympathy
and buoyant encouragement. I need my friends,
in the brightness of whose smiles my weary, care-
worn heart is fed with strength and courage, but
it is still fearfully true that my soul's deepest life
is single and unshared. I live by myself—alone;
alone yet with an indomitable craving for one
with whom to share all that lies nearest and dearest to me; alone, yet urged on always by a vast
fundamental yearning to pour out my heart and
its most secret thoughts and fears and hopes to
someone who will completely understand me.
Friends we have whose love for us is as strong as
our love for them, but friends they are with only
human power to help and so we are alone. Yes,
alone, alone and isolated with a bleak, blank road
to death ahead of us, unless we know the blessed
comradeship of Christ our Lord. He, the sweet
Saviour, who trod the sun-parched roads of Pales-
tine and furrowed the water of Galilee's lake in
quest of souls, has eased, as only He can ease,
this maddening fever of our souls. He knows the

poignant griefs, which lie too deep and cut the heart too keenly for the telling. He knows the inexpressible racking pain of loneliness which beggars all description and He has not left us orphans. He has stayed with us, He dwells with us, that we may come and tell Him all.

A mother may come and tell Him her fears for loved ones, fears that she dare not, cannot, put in words; father can kneel and speak to Him of sharp struggles in the busy markets of the world and of the hungry faces that will all too surely greet him in the near future unless "the Keeper of little ones" quickly lends His aid. Sorrows of heart and fears of mind and terrors of soul, vague forebodings of shadowed days ahead and sharp grief for the hidden sins of days now gone—all may be told Him and we know that the telling will never be taken amiss, will never be misunderstood. But, oh, the solace, when strengthless from the pressure of the cross and speechless with the dread of all that is and all that is to be, we kneel in stricken silence before His tabernacle home. As small children we were wont to show our bruises to our mother and feel relieved if she but gazed on them—and what was mother's gentleness to His!

ॐ

Jesus, knower of the human heart and all its boundless needs, I thank You that You have not left us orphans. It is hard enough at times to see beyond the sacramental veil and catch the sight of Your own dear face, but life would be all too dark, all too dreary and too lonely, if You were not with us now. In Your own good way You have met the deepest need of our lives and, Jesus dear, I need you.

HAPPY AND
FORGETFUL

You had forgotten the eternal God who reared you.

BARUCH 4:8

"Did you ever forget God when you were happy? When I was lonesome, I prayed almost every hour of the day and now it is rather hard to pray; but I must," wrote a young woman whose world was a supremely happy one in the love that had been sanctified a few months before in matrimony. The world was very sweet and in the joy of her young, overflowing heart she penned those words to the teacher who had taught her much about God. She loved God—really, and with her heart —and she was trying hard to serve Him, and yet she knew she was not turning to Him as she once had. "Did you ever forget God when you were happy? . . . now it is rather hard to pray, but I must." Fortunately for her, she realized that such forgetfulness was wrong and still more fortunately she made the resolve not to continue it.

"Did you ever forget God when you were happy?" would be a good question to ask ourselves. And how many of us could answer "No"? When sickness came and darkened the days of one we loved, we went down on our knees and prayed with Martha and Mary: "Lord, he whom Thou lovest is sick." Our prayer was both long and earnest. When men's tongues began to wag and they said unkind things about us, injuring us in our work and hampering our efforts, we were quick to beg protection from God. Yes, let but the slightest cloud veil the sunlight of our lives and like disappointed children we rushed to Him and implored His help. We needed Him badly then and we ran to Him.

But, children that we are, when all went well we forgot God, even as a child forgets mother when it is time to play. We did not feel the need of Him then. Our hearts beat fast with a happiness that seemed to satisfy us adequately and it did for a passing while. Health was ours and all the buoyancy it brings; a sufficiency of the world's wealth offset all fears of a nearing rainy day; and friends were true and most devoted. What was there to ask for? Is it so strange that we failed to run to God?

Strange indeed, strange that we do not go to God like decent people to thank Him for His favors—for life and health and wealth and friends and all the joys that accompany them. Surely a hearty "Thank you, dear Lord" would have been in order. And again: we have these gifts, but have we the power to retain them? Do we not need God's aid to keep the health that is ours, or are we fools enough to think that our refusal to hear would stop death's knocking at our door? The goods of time are ours, but are we really satisfied with our ability to be ultimately successful in a game where the cleverest often lose? Honor may be ours, but others have been cheated of love and praise; and can I protect myself better than they? Yes, it is strange that we forget God, whose watchful protection we need so much each moment of our lives. We really must try to be less impolite with God.

ぐ

Dear Jesus, I know You understand this childish heart of mine. When I stand in need of anything, I always instinctively turn to You because
I know You always want to help me and can always help me. I beg and plead with You and so
You kindly heed my prayer. But, then, off I run
and, when the world smiles, I smile with it and
scarcely think of You. It's not right and I am
ashamed of myself that I treat You in such a
manner. I need you always, Lord, need you badly,
and even if I did not need You, sheer gratitude
ought to make me never forget You.

UPS AND DOWNS

*Lord God, you who are always merciful and
tender-hearted, slow to anger, always loving,
always loyal, turn to me and pity me.*
                                    PSALMS 85:15, 16

A resolution to amend and actual amend-
ment are very distinct and different things. As I
kneel in prayer my mind is flooded with light
and my will is stirred by that same Omnipotence
at whose creative word the world sprang into
being. I see the truths of time and of eternity in
some way as God sees them. I weigh all things in
the scales of God and I find my actions quite unfit
to pass His eye. Then, with an onrush of my will's
full power, I summon up a whole-souled act of
sorrow for the times now gone and pledge myself
to see to it that the past is not repeated in the

future. It is a wholesome act, this breaking in desire with the past, and when we have made it thinkingly and well, then we leave our prayer to go and make our pledge reality. The promise is made, the fulfilment is now to come.

Would it not be well to realize the vital difference between these things? Our resolutions may be strong and very fervent and yet, frail mortals that we are, when the friction of daily life begins to wear and tell on us, we fail in our high resolves. Yesterday, as often before, I told my Master I regretted much all my complaining against His holy will in days gone by and that I really would strive to bear with composure the little trials He would send. Yet, before the day had ended, I was loud in my rebellion once again. This morning I pledged to Christ that I would have done with pride and self-seeking, yet scarcely an hour had gone by when I found myself strutting across life's stage to gain the plaudits of my fellows. And yet I really meant all my morning words. It was the same with charity and with prayer and with all the virtues. Yet, in fairness to myself, I cannot say that I never did resolve to act in a decent manner.

It's distressing, and almost enough to shake any but the bravest hearts. I really love our Lord and I really want to serve Him, but the pull of human nature works against me. It is hard to walk ahead courageously when I know that I fall and rise, only to fall and fall again. It is wearying work this endless righting of myself and it hurts my pride, yes, hurts it very much. Yet, how else can I become a saint and how else can I get to Heaven? I need patience, then, a great deal of patience with myself and a constant thinking on the things of God, until their utter attractiveness so wins my fickle heart that it no longer swerves from the upward path, wandering after creatures and the little comfort they can give.

᪥

O, Jesus, what a tangle of contradictions I am, "one day eager and brave, the next not caring to try," one hour resolving and the next hour acting as though I knew not what a resolution meant! Frankly, it is discouraging, almost too discouraging, until I remember once again that in You and You alone I must find my strength, for "You who are always merciful and tender-hearted, slow to anger, always loving, always loyal." Therefore, I will fight on, dear Lord, fight in the morning, fight in the shadows, fight on because I know my changefulness will be borne with and pitied and one day done away with by my changeless Friend. "Turn to me and pity me."

ENCOURAGEMENT

Take care, brothers, that there is not in any one of your community a wicked mind, so unbelieving as to turn away from the living God. Every day, as long as this "today" lasts, keep encouraging one another so that none of you is hardened by the lure of sin.
HEBREWS 3:12, 13

Mutual encouragement is one of the greatest assets in any walk of life. Our poor human hearts are so fickle and our spirits so prone to droop after a short display of strength that sooner or later we may give up trying. Regardless of what our task in life may be, whether it is making individual progress as a student, training others in our role as mother or teacher, that of the professions or that of the laborer, not many days go by without the inevitable things that weary us. It is then that the companion who stands by our side can strengthen our hearts anew and spur us back into our desired stride, if he but find it in him to say the inspiring word. Encouragement is what most human hearts crave and need.

It is the same in the life of the spirit. To those who really care about their souls, who really find the task of treading the walks of sanctity engrossing, the path steepens often and the music that was in their hearts becomes quite hushed. Then the wish is strong to sink slowly back into the abandoned valley of half-hearted service or at least to stand and make no effort to reach the higher goal. The weight of mortal flesh is all too heavy for the upward path. Just here must come the word that will straighten our shoulders beneath the load and snap our wills back into place. A father, tired of struggling against the sharp practices of the business world, who now feels almost forced to yield to ways and means that God forbids, must hear the voice of her he loves, telling of the land beyond the grave where the just of this world hold forever the wealth of God. A mother worn by willful ways of small children and the seeming ingratitude of growing boys and girls would like to rest from her God-sent task of molding pliant lives; then must father recall the home of Nazareth, where God's own mother did similar work.

Young people begin to find the way of God hard and the music of the world a bit too sweet. Then a true companion must tell them that the narrow way leads back home and the music is the lure to doom. To others, prayer becomes a distasteful task, perseverance in kindly ways of thought and speech and act an irksome chore, fidelity in service to our King a chafing restraint. Oh, then for the friends who will encourage one another every day, "as long as *today* lasts," so long as this mortal life holds men exiles from their true home, bringing once more into bold relief the dimming outlines of eternity, relighting within each other's heart the flickering love of our changeless Friend!

૱

Jesus, the one Friend who ever spurs us on by Your insistent grace, give us earthly friends also to further Your work within our hearts and teach us, too, to do like service unto others. Though Your grace is strong enough, we still at times need a human, audible voice to rouse us, our faintheartedness is so great. So send us inspiring friends and make us be friends to others, for it will mean that Your love will grow much within our hearts.

RESCUED

And where is the god who could save you from my power?

DANIEL 3:15

The king's command had gone forth and all Babylon had obeyed it—all Babylon except the three Jewish young men, Sidrach, Misach and Abdenago. True to their faith, they had refused to fall down in adoration before the king's statue. Die they might, but disobey God they would not. "Then was Nebuchadnezzar filled with fury and the countenance of his face was changed against Sidrach, Misach and Abdenago and he commanded that the furnace should be heated seven times more than it had been accustomed to be heated. And he commanded the strongest men that were in his army to bind the feet of Sidrach, Misach and Abdenago and to cast them into the furnace of burning fire." Helpless, they were hurled into the midst of the flames and the words of the king rang mockingly in their ears: "And where is the god who could save you from my power?"

There seemed to be small hope and yet we know that "the Angel of the Lord went down . . . into the furnace and he drove the flame of the fire out of the furnace and made the midst of the furnace like the blowing of a wind bringing dew, and the fire touched them not at all nor troubled them, nor did them any harm."

What a lesson there is in this miracle! There are times in the lives of all of us when, humanly speaking, hope is utterly gone. All is so dark and so foreboding that everything within and about us cries out despairingly: "And where is the god who could save you from my power?"

It may be that a habit of sin has fastened itself upon us and, though we do want to break away from it, we slip and fall again and again. We would like to find some way out, but we are weak and temptation, when it comes, proves too strong. It is then that the enemy of our souls keeps repeating into our ears: "And where is the god who could save you from my power?" If only he can get us to feel the despair that would be bred in our souls by hearkening to that question, victory is his.

Or it may be that, despite all we try to do, stark poverty seems to lie ahead for ourselves and those we love. The gaunt specter stands in our path. No hope seems left anywhere. Yet, if we but go to Him in whom are hidden the riches of the Godhead and plead our case with Him in full confidence, the tempter will whisper in vain to our souls.

No matter what the crisis is in life, no matter how great the doom that lies ahead, no matter what the crushing sorrow that lies full upon our hearts, if we but go to Him, we shall be safe. We know His mercy and His love better than did the three young men of old and with them, no matter what the darkness of our souls may be, we must answer: "Behold, our God, whom we worship, is able to save us from the furnace of burning fire, and to deliver us out of thy hands, O King. But if He will not, be it known to thee, O King, that we will not worship thy gods, nor adore the golden statue which thou hast set up." Yes, and even more than that, we must find echoing in our hearts the words of Job: "Although He should kill me, I will trust in Him." It is that trust which will steady our souls and bring us peace—and victory.

৵

Dear Jesus, amid all the darkness of this valley of tears I am apt at times to forget Your infinite power and, more than that, Your infinite readiness to help me. My road grows very rough and steep and difficulties beset me so that I would quit the fight and give up all struggling. But would that be right? Would that show confidence in You? You so loved me that You died for me. Shall I not trust You for lesser gifts? Just let my clasping of the crucifix be always my answer, when the tempter cries, "And where is the god who could save you from my power?"

IF ONLY . . . !

Now he has reconciled you, by his death and in that mortal body. Now you are able to appear before him holy, pure and blameless—as long as you persevere and stand firm on the solid base of the faith, never letting yourselves drift away from the hope promised by the Good News.

COLOSSIANS 1:22, 23

Some of us do a great deal of worrying about death and Heaven and hell—all of which is about as profitable as worrying whether the sun will shine tomorrow or not. Obviously, we should be deeply concerned about death and Heaven and hell, but our real and major concern should be about the thing on which they depend, and this is how we live here and now.

Our full accent ought to be on *this* life, or rather on this *day*, this *hour*, this *minute*. A minute is all I have at any time, and any minute may be my last, and on the condition of my soul when my last minute has come will depend my eternity.

If I am driving a car, my concern is not about the hill five miles away but about the curve I am rounding now. If I am at the wheel of a boat, I am not thinking about the billows on the other side of the bay but of the waves just in front of the bow of the boat. It is the present problem that should be solved, not the one that is in the distance.

Why then don't we act in the same way in terms of the life of the soul? On the present depends the future. If I take care of the present the future will take care of itself. Saint Ignatius put it well: "Man is created to know, love, and serve God, and *by so doing*, save his soul." Be concerned about knowing and loving and serving God now—which, in plain English, means merely doing my job in life the way God wants me to— and I need not worry about my soul's salvation.

Saint Paul put it another way. Christ wishes to have us "holy and blameless and irreproachable in His sight" for all eternity. And how will that be brought about? "If only ye hold by the faith, well-grounded and steadfast." If ever a man had both feet on the ground, Saint Paul had, and so his accent is on the "now." He tells me that I shall be holy and blameless and fit to see God face-to-face for all eternity *if only* I know my Faith and adhere to its commands and hold to its practices.

Could anything be more consoling than this doctrine? It is disquieting to think about death and hell, or even Heaven: it seems so unreal and far away. And to think too much about them is to put the accent where it shouldn't be. My present job is to think about the work I have to do now, the prayer I have to say now, the movie I am to see now. It is all so simple: do each moment what I have to do, and when the next moment comes, do what I have to do then; and if some "next moment" the thing to do is die, well, I shall do that the way I did everything else—and I shall wake up in Heaven.

ॐ

Dear Jesus, thank You for this consoling fact of faith and let me daily grow in the realization of its importance. I wish to be with You in Heaven, of course I do. Then what I ought to do is to attend to each present duty and fulfill it as best I can and in the way You wish me to. If I do that always, then, when Your summons comes, I shall be quite ready to come home.

GOD DOES NOT HOLD OUT ON US

But now, now—it is Yahweh who speaks— come back to me with all your heart, fasting, weeping, mourning. Let your hearts be broken, not your garments torn, turn to Yahweh your God again, for he is all tenderness and compassion, slow to anger, rich in graciousness, and ready to relent.

JOEL 2:12, 13

Sometimes our sins stand so vividly before us that they literally strike us in the face.

The sins of our youth and the sins of our maturing years and the sins of the level years and of the years that are sloping downward. Sins of thought and word and deed. Sins of commission and of omission. Sins alone and sins along with others. What a mess it all is! "All my sins rise up before me; all my virtues disappear." And it may be that before that vision our hearts fail within us and we grow quite fearful of God's mercy.

Yes, God is just and His punishment of sin is terrifying. But He punishes only when we force Him, only when we deliberately and willfully refuse to let Him forgive. God never "holds out on us." He wants us to repent and be truly sorry and, the moment we are, He forgives and forgets. Even the grace to repent and to be sorry comes directly and thoughtfully from Him.

It makes no difference what my sins may have been; no matter how vile, no matter how utterly insolent. If we but rend our hearts "in fasting, and in weeping, and in mourning," if we are really sorry, wishing we had not done them, and are really determined now not to do them again, and confess them, as Christ bade us, God being "gracious and merciful, patient and rich in mercy," will forgive the evil we have done and blot it out completely.

But, for most of us, in all frankness, our sins have not been so very heinous. There is no point in painting black blacker. I have sinned, yes, very often, and with scant regard for God's love. I have fumbled life's duties and played free with its privileges; I have acted with scant courtesy toward God in my prayers and have violated the duties of charity toward my neighbor. Where good example should have been given, I have so far failed as not to have led men and women nearer to God. There is little I can be proud of in my life and much, very much, that should make me hang my head in shame. All right! But what then? Not despair, nor discouragement, not a sense of frustration. That would be sheer folly and most untrue of God. The only thing to do is to drop on my knees and cry out from my heart the sorrow that is there—and then await God's grace. And that grace will come as surely as I plead for it and it will work into every nook and cranny of my being, healing and cleansing and strengthening unto a newer life, closer to God.

The worst sin we can commit is ever to suspect that God will "hold out on us" when we come to Him with true sorrow. "A contrite and humble heart, O God, Thou will not despise."

ॐ

Dear Jesus, at times when the past stands out before me in all its sheer sinfulness, my heart grows numb within me and it is all I can do not to give up in despair. By Your grace, I may have been saved from worse sins. But I did sin "in thought, word, and deed." I am sorry now for it all and I ask Your pardon for it all. And I know You will and do forgive, for You never "hold out on us."

A FRIEND'S WISHES

You are my friends, if you do what I command you.

JOHN 15:14

I am always anxious to prove to my friend my love for him. He may be quite sure, and so, too, may I, of the depth and height and breadth of our mutual affection, but show it I must. Now it is a thoughtful word, and now it is a little deed done when the hour is dark, and yet again it is a kindly omission of an act that would offend. I often catch myself daydreaming of new ways that will manifest what I hold so much to heart. And if my friend makes known to me each little thing that pleases him, will words come easily to tell of all my joy? Could trouble or pain or time prevent my giving it to him?

I often want to show my love for our Lord, in fact it is my one enduring thought. I love Him, yes—both He and I are sure of this—yet, as with other friends, I must keep proving it. Would I be pleased to know how I best can give Him joy? Of course I would, and this He knew, and so with thoughtfulness He told me long ago: "You are my friends, if you do what I command you." And what are His commands? To serve Him first and best, because I hold Him dearer than all else. To pray to Him within my home, but best of all to come and chat with Him within His home, wherein He silently waits for me. To count my fellow-man His brother and so to be kind to him in thought, word and deed. To lend a helping hand when others fall and to shore them up when they lean heavily. To count myself of little worth save only when I do His will in every least detail and even then to realize that it is His aiding grace that saves me. To think of Heaven as my real home and earth but as my place of pilgrimage, wherein I prove my right to a welcome home when death summons me. Thus it is He tells me

how my love can show itself. But do I always give
him the gifts He asks?

❦

Dear Jesus, friend whom I love so deeply, I
thank You for Your thoughtfulness. I would have
found it hard to know just how to show my love
for You, for You are great and I am so very small.
Yet love would not endure without some proof.
I thank You for the secret You have told me and
I shall try hard to give You what You want.

A FORGIVING SPIRIT

*Father, forgive them; they do not know
what they are doing.*

LUKE 23:34

Forgiveness of those who have wronged
us is a virtue that costs us much. Revenge holds
out to us such a sense of satisfaction and the spite-
ful words promise so adequate a balm to our
wounded feelings! Then, too, does not a proper
respect for our rights, as men and women, demand that we put the offenders abruptly back
into their place and give them much to think
about concerning their own ill-trained characters?
Isn't it the time for someone—and who better
than we ourselves?—to place straying feet back on
the straight and narrow path from which they
have so evidently wandered?

When we feel thus and would speed on our
errand of would-be charity, let us stop for just one
moment in the home of our Friend to ask Him

what He thinks of our purpose. He will not keep us waiting. "My child, what did I, your Friend and Leader, do, when My own people had nailed Me to the cross and were hurling blasphemies and curses at Me as I hung dying before their gaze? Will you go now and act in otherwise? And you, too, my child! I forgave thee all the debt, because thou besoughtest Me; shouldst not thou then have had compassion on thy fellow-servant, even as I had compassion on thee?"

Shall we? There will be no less manhood in us when we have done what the Son of God did so repeatedly. We shall have lost no self-respect by stamping our souls with the image of Him who was the most perfect of men. The fleeting satisfaction of having stung our brother in return, the questionable pleasure of showing him what faults we find that he possesses, these will not be ours. No, thank God, they will not. But in their stead the consciousness of a soldier's part well played, the joy of having followed Christ when "the lead" was hard and our nature stoutly rebelled, yes, and deep down within our souls the new-won grace of God, by which we claim a higher place in Heaven throughout eternity because of the little victory we have won. Can there be question of a hesitant choice?

ॐ

Jesus, oh, how glad I am that I have paused to ask You what You thought and how You looked on what I wished to do! The tempest of hurt feelings was surging in my soul and would have struck back in my anger. But you have shown me where true knighthood lay and how my soul could grow more like Your own. I thank you

for the lesson, O my God, and I beg Your grace
to make my life like unto Yours.

LOVED

*I have shown love for you, says Yahweh.
But you ask, "How have you shown your
love?"*

MALACHI 1:2

It was a dark hour for the Jews and their
enemies were pressing them hard from all sides.
Each day brought its sorrow and trial, each day
the shadows darkened and the problems deep-
ened, until utter desperation seemed the logical
sentiment for all. Then it was that God, through
His prophet, spoke to them of His love and told
them how near and dear they were to Him. "I
have shown love for you," said the Lord. And
they answered Him: "How have you shown your
love?" They forgot Egypt and Sinai and the mir-
acle-fed years in the desert and the day that Jor-
dan stood asunder and the evening when the sun
went not down in Ajalon. They forgot Hebal and
Garizim where the twelve tribes stood and swore
to love and serve their God for all His loving
kindness to them. They forgot it all and cried:
"How have you shown your love?"

Can we not catch more than a faint resem-
blance to ourselves in this? When joy is in our
lives we are quite willing to admit God's love for
us, but when the shadows fall, what then? I had
dreamed a dream for years and just when it
should come true, it vanishes into thin air. The

little child God gave to cheer life's hours with
laughter has now had its lips closed in death
and all the merry noise is hushed. The hard-
earned savings of days when I labored and toiled
and stinted myself against the leaner years are
swept away from me and I find myself facing
life's downgrade with scant assurance of my live-
lihood. I have sought hard to fight the battles of
life in the right manner and to play my part as
a man should play it, and now I find myself
quite helpless on a bed of pain or crippled. Then
someone comes and tells me of God's love for me
and tries to lift my eyes beyond the darkened
present. What do I say then? Is all the past for-
fotten? Do I complain, "How have you shown
your love?" How? What of the gift of life itself
and the gift of warming sun and cooling evening! What of the gifts of bird and beast and
flower! What of the gifts of the Church, of Bap-
tism, Confirmation, Penance—of the greatest gift
of all, the gift of His own Self to be my food!
"How have you shown your love?" Roll back the
scroll of time, slowly, very slowly, for every moment was His gift and each hour came endowed
with His graces, and when I have unrolled it,
can I then ask "How have you shown your love?"

ॐ

Dear Jesus, changeless lover of my soul, please
never let the darkness grow so great that I lose
sight of all Your love. You know how prone I
am to lose it. You had Your hour of shadowed
agony in Gethsemane and again upon the Cross
and then it was You deigned to feel the dreadful
depths of my poor soul's darknesses. Just help me,
Lord, to take the crosses as I take the joys of life

and grant that I remember always wherein You have loved me.

HURT FEELINGS

A man's shrewdness shows in equanimity, his self-respect in overlooking an offense.
PROVERBS 19:11

"If they only gave you credit for being thoughtful," said the man who had planned and schemed to serve others' moods and desires only to be completely misunderstood. He had studied their times of work and their hours of leisure, had worked out as best he could the tangles of their character and then adjusted and readjusted with patience the work in which many were needed to cooperate. Yet, when all was done, some were offended because they felt they were treated inconsiderately.

Hurt feelings are the cause of so many quarrels and feelings are hurt so very often because we imagine that others have been inconsiderate. We are so far within our own focus that we ourselves bulk out of all proportion to every other object in the world. When all mankind does not dance in attendance, or when we think they have failed in any way to show us proper respect and required honor, we immediately become outraged.

Isn't it a pity? There is so much great work to be done in this world and so little time to do it in that it is a sad, sad thing to waste precious moments nursing our imagined woes. But suppose we are really slighted! Are we not bigger men

and women when we rise high enough to be able
to stoop very low? What earthly use is there in
carrying quivering nerves through life to rasp our
own souls and cause irritation in others?

Slights do come, but, most often, much is due
to our imaginings. Sensitive and wincing at every
touch that does not come most gently, we sense
a slur where none was intended and feel a hurt
that was never inflicted. Does that help life—
our own and others—to be more smooth and gracious? Surely it does not. Then why not try to
tuck our feelings away and keep the even tenor
of our lives, not getting pained at every con-
tact?

ॐ

Dear Jesus, how much good is spoiled in my
own life and in the lives of others by my hurt
feelings. I grow peevish and quite out of sorts
when others pass me by or merely seem to overlook me, and then my work suffers and perhaps
even my health, if my sensitivity reaches undue
bounds. It is all a pity, Lord; so help me to
get over it! Children fret at everything, but I am
supposed to be full-grown. So give me grace to
take life, as it is, manfully and not to give way
so frequently to hurt feelings.

INTERESTED
IN OTHERS

*Have they made you president? Do not let
it go to your head, behave like everyone else
in the party, see that they are happy and
then sit down yourself.*

ECCLESIASTICUS 32:1

"He's not interested. That's all." This
was the answer given to the young man who was
complaining that his superior never asked about
the health of anyone, never said a word of praise,
never made a remark except to point out a flaw.
There was no positive unkindness, but there was
never the slightest interest in what those under
him were doing, never an interest in their aims
or ambitions. And that was hard for all, but dou-
bly hard for someone who by nature needed to realize that somebody did care.

One may retort that it was a "defect of character." Perhaps. But then it is a defect that is
very prevalent and one from which very few are
entirely free. We are by nature social beings and
meant to live in one another's company. Inevitably, this supposes that we are to have a due regard for their opinions and expect them to have a
like regard for ours. Rare is the man or woman
who does not care what others think.

What is harder than for a husband to feel
that nothing he does is of the slightest interest
to his wife; that she takes so little interest in it
that he might just as well be a complete stranger?

And if a wife feels that all her attempts to please, all her efforts to think out the problems of the home, are passed by unnoticed, what a wrenching of the heart there is!

Children may feel that parents are glad to be rid of them and pack them off to bed and then in their later years send them on to boarding school just in order to "get them out of the way." Yet, the parents should be standing in the place of God and they are the ones who should visibly manifest to the children God's loving Providence over them.

The story is the same in school or in the office. The consciousness that work well done is noticed, that faults, while not overlooked, are not the only things that are noticed, that a decent regard is had for the human dignity of each and every man, woman or child—that and that alone will create a spirit of loyalty, an atmosphere of contentment, an eagerness to study or to work.

No matter where I am, no matter how humble my position in life, there will always be a chance for me to take an interest in others. If my position is one of authority, especially an authority whose mainspring is supposedly that of loyalty or love, then my clear duty is to be interested and the scope of my influence very broad and very deep.

ॐ

Dear Lord, the one great privilege in life is to help others. We all need at least the help of encouragement and that costs very little, yet is valued so much. My field of influence may not be very wide but I do want to do all the good that I can. So I shall try to make all those over whom I am placed feel that I am properly interested in them and their work and all that happens to them.

A FRANK FRIEND

They dress my people's wound without concern; Peace! Peace! they say, but there is no peace.

JEREMIAH 8:11

We all need a friend who will be brutally frank with us. Try as we may to examine ourselves, we can never know ourselves accurately by unaided self-analysis. We are too far within focus to see ourselves in proper perspective and our known motives color our actions too distinctly for us to discover clearly the more hidden and radical sources of our general run of actions.

Nor is it a true friend who soothes our soul by assuring us that "All is well," that "Things are going fine," that we "are great." It was in that way that the false prophets and priests acted centuries ago to the people of Jerusalem, who were steeped in idolatry. Many did not realize the wrongness of their ways. Those who should have awakened them failed to do so and taught them to cry: "We are wise and the law of the Lord is with us." Yet, in truth, the law was far from them and so God sent them Jeremiah, who pitilessly pleaded with them to return to God. He did not heal "the breach of the daughter of God's people disgracefully." Nor did he cry "Peace, peace." He told them plainly that "there is no peace," for the anger of God was upon them.

If God has given me such a friend, I should thank Him very much, for then and then only can I grow daily to proper maturity and advance in saintliness. If I have no such friend, with His help I must seek and find one.

It may be one to whom I lay bare the hidden recesses of my soul as best I can and let him read therein the meaning of my temperament and character. And when he has untangled the skeins and has told me what manner of man I am, I shall listen humbly and profit by his advice.

It may be a friend who goes, side by side, through life with me. He knows my comings-in and my goings-out, my likes and my dislikes, my thought-out actions and my instinctive ones. Reading between all these lines, my friend will catch the hidden meanings that betray now this good quality, now that bad trait.

To listen to such a friend is not the most pleasant thing in the world; but why, to escape the hurt, would I want the breaches of my soul to be healed disgracefully?

ॐ

Dear Lord, try as I may I cannot know myself with satisfying adequacy. Yet, without such knowledge I can never smooth off the rough edges of character, nor develop to the full the good qualities I have. So grant me, please, a true, frank friend who will show me my soul as it is so that I may daily grow more pleasing in Your sight.

THE END IS LONG
IN COMING

The man who stands firm to the end will be saved.

MATTHEW 10:22

"Heaven comes at the end, but the end is long in coming," Saint Bernadette Soubirous is reported to have remarked as her failing strength brought her slowly to the grave. Even if she did not actually say it, it is much in line with other things she did say. Years back, at Lourdes grotto, the "Lady" had promised her happiness "not in this world but in the next." That was twenty-one years before and those twenty-one years had brought their share of suffering, physical, mental and spiritual. "Heaven comes at the end" had cheered her always, and yet, as the years passed slowly with their weight of pain, her human heart, despite the vision before her, must have kept on saying, "The end is long in coming."

How often do we not cry out as Bernadette did! We know "Heaven comes at the end," we know that God has laid up treasures for us for all eternity and that no man can even dimly glimpse what will be our happiness at home with Him forever. But the clouds grow darker and the darkness comes on and the vision is blurred. It is hard to push on, reaching a steadying hand to rest upon the future that seems to be as distant today as it was yesterday. And then the thought may well come: Is it all a mirage? Are we just

103

plain fools counting on a future that never comes?

Father and mother may feel that way when they face a future made black and bare by the ungratefulness of children. Friend may have known and loved friend, and life's path may have been less fatiguing because of mutual aid; but now friendship's bond is sundered and life's path must be traveled alone. And never did the way seem so wearing and so long.

The young are told to keep their lives clean and fresh and pure and that when God comes to seal all with His final judgment the clean of heart will be very near and dear to Him. But that judgment is far away and the world of sin is an appealing one that finds full response in newly awakened lives.

For some, the years have brought more than their share of sorrow and pain and yet there seems to be no surcease. The vision of Heaven has been kept bright over many dark days, but it may grow hard for dimming eyes to catch it afresh as before.

"But the end is long in coming." And God knows we find it hard to tarry till He comes. And so He understands and will have patience with our impatience and asks only that we too have patience with ourselves—and with Him.

ॐ

Dear Jesus, thanks to You I am assured that "Heaven comes at the end." And for that sure knowledge I am very grateful. But it comes only at the end, and often I get so tired of trying, so weary of plodding ahead in the dark. I know I ought to keep the vision bright, but when darkness comes and pain afflicts me, it is very hard. And then it seems to be so dreadfully true that "the end is long in coming." But, Jesus, stand by me, please, in just those hours when the vision is dimmed, and hold my hand lest I stray, for I do want to keep on the way to Heaven, no matter how far it be away.

A CONSTANT VISITOR

Happy the man who listens to me, who day after day watches at my gates to guard the portals.

PROVERBS 8:34

Our hearts are hungry for friendship with the good, the noble and the true. There is a craving within us, which only years of lowest degradation can banish, for friends whose every word and work may lead us one step nearer the ideal of our lives. We may seem very self-sufficient in many lines. We may be sought by our fellow-men for cheer and heartening in their manifold trials, but each of us is in need of an inspiring friend. Here we seek him and there our quest leads us on and most of us know the poignancy of fruitless search. Such friends are few and far between and perhaps we wander always in the intervening wasteland alone.

But this need not be, nor, even if we have happily missed the loneliness of isolated ways, have we to rest our tiring weight on human shoulders only. Noble friends are good, of course, very good, but there are times when the noblest of them is but a broken staff, a helpless fellow-exile. They bow before the burden of their own great cross or maybe there is no human strength that can lift the cross we bear. Then it is that he is blessed who has learned to watch daily at the gates of the home of Christ and waits at His doors. To school myself just to turn aside and steal but a hurried moment to greet my changeless Friend, who is ever listening for my footsteps on His threshold, will bring new sunshine into my shadow-filled life. Most cheering of friends, most secretive of confidants, I may run in to have just one word with Him, but when I leave, somehow I see the sunshine now and not the shadows, somehow I find a music in my heart that is but the echo of cheering words I heard Him speak therein. A moment's tarrying and yet my heart unburdened itself, a moment's tarrying and yet my cross was lifted or else my Friend gave new courage to bear a burden He would have me carry a little while longer. Thus it is each day whether sunshine or shadow play upon my heart and then the day comes, as come it always does, when storm-clouds break and I find myself aghast at what seems to be the coming wreckage of my life. Then it is that our Lord will hear me drag my leaden steps within His home and see me throw myself before Him in full terror at the storm. Yet my heart will have an unshaken confidence that, as of old, so in these later days, His words can stay the winds and waves, though they are high as mountains.

꒰꒱

Dear Lord, no man can know what Your Real Presence means, save only he who comes and watches daily at Your gates and waits at Your doors. No other comfort is there in this land of tears that approaches it, whether it be a joy or a sorrow that moves our souls. To You I come, to You I tell my heart's own story, from You in ways which You alone could tell I draw fresh courage for life's battles. "For, though I should walk in the midst of the shadow of death I fear no evils, for Thou are with me, Thy rod and Thy staff, they have comforted me."

SEEKING HELP RIGHTLY

I am thirsty.
JOHN 19:28

We sometimes deem it a decided weakness to let another know of our interior suffering, whether it be of body or of mind. Should we not be strong enough to bear it alone and to whisper no least word to anyone? Would it not be wiser, nobler, to act in that way? Well, it may be in itself, but for most of us there is a true need to talk it all out with someone, to tell someone of our pains and our sorrows, even though we know beforehand that there can be no lifting of the cross.

That tendency is rooted in our very nature and

may we not say that our Lord sanctioned and put
His all-wise approval on it when He cried out on
the cross, "I am thirsty"? He sought no relief, for
there was none save in the drugged wine with
which He would not dull His pain; but was it not
good of our Lord to show us this truly human
trait that in His agony He would cry out His
suffering? He suffered long in silence to show us
that it is very good that we bear all patiently and
without murmur; and even when He did call out
in His agony, there was no complaining, no rebellion, no pleading for false sympathy.

Let us take our trials to the Lord, of course;
always, and first and last. Let us look to Him and
Him alone for the ultimate help of His grace
without which all other help proves but a broken
reed. But let us remember, too, that we can, yes
and at times should, show the wounds of soul
and body to some kind friend in God, who will
lead us gently but firmly back to the same dear
Friend to whom we have gone of ourselves. Pent-
up sorrow or shut-up pain gnaws away at body
and soul and it helps a great deal to pour it all
out into a willing ear.

Only let us be certain that we tell our trial to
a friend in God and of God, not to the worldly-
minded who would have us drown it all out with
the music and pleasures that sweep us out of
ourselves into a witless way of living. Not to
rebellious men who, like the wife of Job, would
have us curse God and die. Not to the proud who,
counting not on God's grace, will throw us back
on our own willpower and have us grin and bear
it in the manner of a pagan. No, to none of these,
but to one who is at home with the things of
God, whose mind is attuned to the thoughts of

God, whose will does really strive to be in unison with God.

❧

Dear Jesus, I am glad You have taught me that it is well not to keep my load of sorrow to myself and to stumble ahead unaided. I know I must come to You if I am to be really helped and yet I realize that, knowing this poor heart of mine, You will be glad to have me tell my crosses to another pilgrim in the vale of tears, another pilgrim who has learned to carry crosses, too, by looking up and beyond the mists that cloud our vision here to our home above. And I would ask You to send me such a friend always, that my weary and perhaps wavering steps may be led more surely back to You.

I HOPE I DIE BEFORE YOU

In your old age I shall be still the same, when your hair is grey I shall still support you. I have already done so, I have carried you. I shall still support and deliver you.
ISAIAH 46:4

"Well, I hope I die before you do. Life would be too hard without your support."

Thus spoke one friend to the other. He really meant it, even though it might sound foolish or sentimental. He had learned to lean heavily on his friend, for his road through life had always been

a hard one and the shadows were long and dark.
Push ahead he might so long as he was conscious
of his friend's nearness and ready help. But the
future would be too bleak and too forbidding
were that friend gone.

That thought of dreaded isolation has come
to many of us with all its chilling fear. Each one
of us needs help in some way or another. We
may be strong intellectually, yet need the support
of another to make us morally strong. Moral
strength may be ours, and yet we may find another's help is necessary to carry the cross of im-
paired bodily vigor.

All earthly friends we may lose, and yet an
abiding friend we must have—one who will be
with us tomorrow and tomorrow's morrow—on
until earth's pilgrimage is ended.

And God has met that need.

My best Friend will never leave me, can never
cease to be my Friend. Life may run on for only
a few days or a few weeks more—He will be with
us. It may stretch out over years—He will be with
us still. At home or in strange lands—there He
will be at our sides. In youth or old age, in
times of gladness or of sorrow, in riches or in
poverty—no matter. He will be with us always and
everywhere.

For "even in your old age I shall still be the
same, when your hair is grey I shall still support
you." Never need I fear to lose Him—except by
sin. And even then, I may regain His friendship
at once, if only I will to have it again.

᳖

Dear Jesus, You have been very, very good to
me to be my changeless Friend, one who will

never, can never, leave me. I fear the loss of earthly friends upon whom I lean heavily. Some are gone already. Others may go—and then! You know the loneliness of it all, the sense of helplessness that grips me in my isolation. Yes, You know it so well that You have given me Yourself to be my Friend —today, tomorrow and up to the hour of death. Thank you, Lord, for being my changeless Friend here and may You be such for all eternity.

GOD'S

But now, thus says Yahweh, who created you, Jacob, who formed you, Israel: Do not be afraid, for I have redeemed you; I have called you by your name, you are mine.
ISAIAH 43:1

The fundamental loneliness and insufficiency of each individual human life is well shown in the fact that we all want to "belong" to something or someone. To stand and face life alone is the starkest trial in all life's many problems. So we join with others and seek their companionship. We "belong" to a club, to a literary group, to a bridge club, to an athletic association. We give ourselves a "cause" and labor with others in seeking to promote it. We seek enduring, intimate friendships and, when this need of other human love is strong, we give our lives each to each in the highest terms of human love, the marriage bond. Then in real truth each belongs to the other, rounding out their individual selves.

For others, the sense of loneliness and inadequacy is just as real and just as poignant, but by God's grace they face life without the joys of human love that they may work for God alone. For to them as "to the tribe of Levi he gave no possession, because the Lord, the God of Israel, Himself is their possession."

But whether we travel through life accompanied by shared and sharing human love or without it, for each of us the deepest depths of our craving to "belong" to something or someone other than ourselves can be adequately satisfied by one and one alone: God. Truly we do belong to Him, in so real and necessary a sense that God himself could not have us not belong to Him. His right of ownership is worked into the very fibers of our being and we simply could not exist unless we were His. From the very moment we came into existence on through time and unending eternity we are His. We belong to Him and He himself cannot give us away to another.

"You are mine." And so whether human love be rightly mine or whether I have freely deprived myself of it for God, the loneliness and inadequacy of my poor self has been met by God. Small I am, yes, but I belong to Infinity; unwise I am, but I belong to Omniscience; weak and frail I am, but Omnipotence guards me. Apart I am and sundered from all others in the deepest things of life, but He has created and formed me and no least corner of my being can be hidden from His eyes.

"You are mine"! I belong to God, and that gives a meaning to life that makes it really worth while. I belong to God, and that gives me a sense of security that robs life of its fears and death of its terrors. I belong to God, and that spurs me into knowing and loving and serving Him as the only One truly worthy of the best that is in me.

ॐ

Dear Jesus, what a consolation it is to know that I belong to You, wholly and irrevocably. Other human loves may be mine, but that does not satisfy completely even when given unstintingly. And so it means everything to belong to You. Only Your infinite Self can satisfy this craving which You yourself have crowded into my small self. Thanks, dear Lord, for making me Yours.

SADNESS
NOT FOR MAN

The vine has withered, the fig tree wilts away; pomegranate, and palm, and apple, every tree in the field is drooping. Yes, gladness has faded among the sons of men.
JOEL 1:12

Sadness was never made for man. God crowned His creation with a creature, made to His own image and likeness and in God the light is never darkened by shadows. Thus would God have man. The light of the sun is to cheer and guide his mortal feet and the light of God's grace and supernatural friendship to throw unflickering rays on the path would lead his immortal soul back home. Darkness there may be for the soul, even as night falls on the body, but both darknesses were meant for respite, not for irritation.

This is the ailing of many a soul. When God in His wisdom is kind enough to shed refreshing darkness, we read things quite amiss and then "gladness has faded among the sons of men." Death comes to those we love and we let the shadows lengthen out across our lives and grieve as those that have no hope. Sickness strikes and we tug hard at its unwelcome bonds. A disappointment here, a setback there, and there again the vanishing of long-kept dreams leave a blight upon our souls and the fruit of our virtues is no more. Yet it could and should be otherwise. The shadows that fall upon our lives must leave them sweet and smiling as the shading of the passing cloud upon the hills' green slopes. With the eyes of faith, we look about and above and beyond, until we see God's grace so manifoldly on our lives that we smile on the gathering clouds and our hearts beat on merrily when all the way seems dark and drear.

And why not? There is One always by our side to pour this oil of gladness into our hearts and to dry the tears before they ever fall, One whose love knows no overclouding, into whose welcoming presence we can always hurry and hear the Voice that was music to Mary's ears and kept joy there even beneath the Cross.

ॐ

Jesus, Giver of all good gifts, give me the joyousness of Your saints. It means so much to keep Your sunlight in my heart and I am so prone to miss the silver lining of the clouds You send my way. I am a foolish child, without a child's glad heart. But make me a happy-hearted child and keep me so in all the darkness of this life until the morning of Heaven comes and in the morning You will "wipe away all tears from our eyes and death shall be no more, nor mourning, nor crying, nor sorrow shall be any more, for the former things are passed away."

INDISPENSABILITY

When you have done all you have been told to do, say, "We are merely servants: we have done no more than our duty."

LUKE 17:10

Someone who had a keen sense of humor deftly caught the self-importance we all are at times prone to feel:

Farewell! I'm fading, cried
    a hailstone, earthward pelted;
How will the earth abide
    without me, when I'm melted?

It's a funny thought, of course, but are we not just as funny when we take ourselves too seriously?

Unless I am quite worthless, it would be foolish for me to deny that I am doing some good or am of some real value. Humility does not consist in lying, even to oneself. But no matter what I am doing, and no matter what position I may hold, and no matter how indispensable I may

seem to be, the solid truth is that one of these
days this world is going to get along without me,
just as it got along without me during many a
long day in the past. And to think that no other
human being can take my place or fill it adequately is sheer self-delusion.

This should be a curb on any pride and a
sobering thought when my forward position or
the praise of men would entice me to strut about
on life's stage. "How will the world abide without me, when I'm melted?"

To my own little circle I may be of definite
help and for them and with them I should do all
the good I can. They need me and I should do
wrong to stint them. Yet all the while, as I labor,
I must keep my poise and my conviction that, if
and when I go, God will still protect that group
of near and dear ones.

Among the larger group of men and women
my influence may be exerted through printed or
spoken word and it may rightly be that many are
helped over life's hurdles by my counsels. But
other tongues have been stilled and other pens
laid aside and yet the world survived.

Will this discourage me or numb my energies?
Not if I have a proper sense of values or look
down the corridors of time into eternity as God
does. Rather, it will spur me into action that
here and now I may do all the good I can for
"the night cometh, when no man can work."

ह➳

Dear Jesus, I am apt to have a distorted sense
of my importance. Certainly there is work for
which You have deigned to need me and that I
must do and I want to do it. But let me not

exaggerate my work or think myself indispensable. That is a sad state of mind. I will try, dear
Lord, to work hard for You and to do all the good
I can for You, realizing all the time that I am by
no means indispensable.

THANK GOD,
I KNEW HIM!

*[Dorcas] never tired of doing good or giving
in charity. But the time came when she got
ill and died, and they washed her and laid
her out in a room upstairs. . . . All the
widows stood round [Peter] in tears, showing him tunics and other clothes Dorcas had
made when she was with them.*
ACTS 9:36–39

The old priest lay dead. Far away, a young
man waited for the message that would tell him
that all was over. It came and he went down the
street to the neighboring church in order that he
might pray for the man of God who had helped
him over so many rough spots in life. But, when
he had entered and knelt to pray, before all else
the words came straight from his heart: "Dear
Lord, thank You for his friendship! Thank You
that I knew the man, for he brought me nearer
to You." Then, and only then, did he pray that
God's mercy would be plentiful in pardoning whatever was amiss in the life that was over.

What a thought for each of us! Suppose I were
to die this minute, would any kneel down and

forcefully thank God that they had known me?
Would they swiftly think of this, even before
they had thought to pray for my soul?

Mother lies in death and around her father
and children kneel. As they look back over the
years, despite all their sorrow, is there a deep,
abiding joy that she was wife and mother to them,
because of her vital nearness to God? Father has
folded tired hands and the roar of the world is
hushed for him now. Does mother thank God
from her heart that years back she placed her hand
in his "for better, for worse—until death do us
part"? Do son and daughter feel that they "are
the children of the saints" and that father's care
over them was but an image of God's care?

A teacher has laid aside the books and closed
the desk for the last time. As pupils come to bid
a last farewell, is there a conscious sense of loss,
a realization that the one who has now gone home
to God always looked on them as young friends
to be led by word and, far more, by example, to
know and love and serve Him better?

A friend has died and as the mourners come
does each one go back over the years and find
here a kindly word and there a helping hand—
and everywhere the wordless exhortation of a life
that lifted them up to higher things?

Again, I ask myself: If I were to die now,
what? The answer can be clearly read, if only I
have the eyes to see it. Let me look to my daily
actions and see how they affect the lives of others.
Let me listen to my words and put myself in the
place of my listeners and ask myself would I be
helped or hindered by such words. Let me look
to the ideals I harbor in my mind, for they are
being slowly but surely stamped out on my char-

acter. Are these ideals high and holy? If so, when I am gone, men will thank God that they have known me. If not . . .

ॐ

Dear Jesus, I should like to leave a rich heritage of holy memories when I am gone. To have so lived that men and women will be the better for my brief presence is a desire I ought always to keep fresh in my heart. I want it to be so. I want my life to be such that, through it and by it, each one I meet will be drawn nearer unto You. And so, let me live each day in thought and word and deed, that all will thank You that they have known me.

OTHER RESOURCE MATERIALS

MY CHANGELESS FRIEND by Francis Le Buffe, S.J., Updated by Catharine Hughes. The first of a planned series drawn from this great spiritual author who began writing in the *Messenger of the Sacred Heart* under this title. The second volume is *Friends Aren't Kept Waiting.*

—$1.45, Paper

THE GOSPEL OF THE HOLY SPIRIT by Alfred P. McBride, O. Praem. A popular study edition of the Acts of the Apostles which dramatizes the permeating presence of the Holy Spirit in the primitive Church of Peter and Paul. Father McBride's commentary underlines the striking parallel—of disagreements, tensions, and dissatisfaction—of those early days with the turmoil following Vatican II.

—$1.50, Paper (Resource Guide, 75¢)

GENESIS REGAINED by F. J. Sheed. The highly respected publisher-author-editor-street preacher here provides the modern reader with insights into the Book of Genesis—with authority, humor, and awareness of the major influences on even the most sophisticated person's mentality today.

—$4.95, Cloth

THEOLOGY AND SANITY by F. J. Sheed. This book has become a classic for its clear, concise analysis of the role of God in the lives of modern men and women.

—$3.50, Cloth

PASSING IT ON by James Ewens, S.J. A guide for today's concerned parents for teaching the Faith to their children. With an appreciation of the author's success in helping mothers and fathers to understand the needs of their offspring by Dr. Christiane Brusselmans. Here is a straightforward presentation of the psychological and real-life influences parents must comprehend before assuming their rightful roles as the prime religious educators of their children.

—$1.75, Paper

THE EXPLOSION OF THE SUPERNATURAL by John Haffert. A review of recent spiritual phenomena, including the growing effect of the charismatic and pentecostal movements and the impact of religious manifestations on the spiritual lives of men and women of our times.

—$1.95, Paper

Cassette Tapes

ADAM AND EVE AND US. Frank Sheed, here recorded for the first time in studio conditions, gives his insightful views of the Book of Genesis in a style even the most sophisticated listener will appreciate. Tasteful humor and homely examples from contemporary developments enhance the presentation.
—$29.95, 4 cassettes (2 hours) with 12-page resource guide

HOW TO PRAY—Bernard Bassett, S.J. A world-famous preacher and retreat master perceptively guides American listeners to teach themselves to pray. Humorous but serious, the tapes provide a personal source for study, guidance, and inspiration.
—$19.95, 2 cassettes (2 hours)

WHAT'S GOING ON IN THE CHURCH? Author-publisher Frank Sheed, adult education leader Mary Reed Newland, and theologian Dr. Anthony Padovano dialogue here on key questions of the times, directed by Father Arthur P. McNally, C. P., associate editor of *Sign* magazine. Each makes a statement which is then discussed by all. Key topics are: "Why Be a Catholic?", "Prayer," "What Christ Means to Me," and "The Church—Who's Minding It?"
—$29.95, 4 cassettes (4 hours)

A Special Offer

THE NEW AMERICAN BIBLE, Christian Life Edition. "The most beautiful Bible in 500 years." The perfect family Bible with the official translation of the readings of the Mass. Gilt-edged, beautifully decorated, gold-stamped padded cover, 1516 pages, 8⅜" x 10¼". Personal and Family Record pages. 85 color pages of Michelangelo's works. Basic reference material of special interest to practicing Catholics and inspirational features. Full money-back guarantee.
—$21.95 (Publisher's price $39.95. You save $18.00)

Order Your Resource Materials Today From—